A JOURNEY OF RICHES

Facing your Fears

11 Insights To Help You Confront Anything

Published by Motion Media International
Editing: Gwendolyn Parker, Chris Drabenstott, and Daniel Decillis
Cover Design: Motion Media International
Typesetting & Assembly: Motion Media International
Printing: Amazon and Ingram Sparks
Creator: John Spender - Primary Author
Title: A Journey Of Riches - Facing your Fears

ISBN Digital: 978-1-925919-20-2
ISBN Print: 978-1-925919-21-9

Subjects: Self-Help, Motivation/Inspiration and Spirituality.

Acknowledgments

Reading and writing is a gift that very few give to themselves. It is such a powerful way to reflect and gain closure from the past; reading and writing is a therapeutic process. The experience raises one's self-esteem, confidence, and awareness of self.

I learned this when I collated the first book in the A Journey Of Riches series, which now includes twenty two books with over 230 different co-authors from more than forty different countries. It's not easy to write about your personal experiences and I honor and respect every one of the authors who have collaborated in the series thus far.

For many of the authors, English is their second language, which is a significant achievement in itself. In creating this anthology of short stories, I have been touched by the amount of generosity, gratitude, and shared energy that this experience has given everyone.

The inspiration for A Journey of Riches, Facing your Fears was a suggestion from a previous author in the series Sharee Siva. Sharee contributed to book four in the series Dealing with Change. She wanted to collaborate again and she felt confronting ones fear was a worthy topic. My sincere thanks to Sharee. Naturally, I could not have created this book without the ten other co-authors who all said YES when I asked them to share their insights and wisdom. Just as each chapter in this book makes for inspiring reading, each story represents one chapter in the life of each of the authors, with the chief aim of having you, the reader, living a more inspired life. Together we can overcome our fears and live a more fulfilling existence.

I want to thank all the authors for entrusting me with their unique memories, encounters, and wisdom. Thank you for sharing and opening the door to your soul so that others may learn from your experience. I trust the readers will gain confidence from your successes, and also wisdom, from your failures.

I also want to thank my family. I know you are proud of me, seeing how far I have come from that 10-year-old boy who was learning how to read and write at a basic level. Big shout out to my Mom, Robert, Dad, Merril; my brother Adam and his daughter Krystal; my sister Hollie, her partner Brian, my nephew Charlie and niece, Heidi; thank you for your support. Also, kudos to my grandparents, Gran and Pop, who are alive and well, and Ma and Pa, who now rest in peace. They accept me just the way I am with all my travels and adventures around the world.

Thanks to all the team at Motion Media International; you have done an excellent job at editing and collating this book. It was a pleasure working with you on this successful project, and I thank you for your patience in dealing with the various changes and adjustments along the way.

Acknowledgments

Thank you, the reader, for having the courage to look at your life and how you can improve your future in a fast and rapidly changing world.

Thank you again to my fellow co-authors: Nicole Seeger, Susan Dampier, Matt Bruce, Dr. Colleen Sabol-Olitsky, Jan Desmet, Carol Williams, Tracy Sotirakis, Nicolas Perrin, Jayma Lyn G. Day, and Peggy Liling Chen.

We would greatly appreciate an honest review on Amazon if this book inspires you. This is how we gain more readers to our inspiring book!

With gratitude
John Spender

Praise for *A Journey of Riches* book series

"The A Journey of Riches book series is a great collection of inspiring short stories that will leave you wanting more!"
~ Alex Hoffmann, Network Marketing Guru.

"If you are looking for an inspiring read to get you through any change, this is it!! This book is comprised of many gripping perspectives from a collection of successful international authors with a tone of wisdom to share."
~ Theera Phetmalaigul, Entrepreneur/Investor.

"A Journey of Riches is an empowering series that implements two simple words in overcoming life's struggles.

By diving into the meaning of the words "problem" and "challenge," you will find yourself motivated to believe in the triumph of perseverance. With many different authors from all around the world coming together to share various stories of life's trials, you will find yourself drenched in encouragement to push through even the darkest of battles.

The stories are heartfelt personal shares of moving through and transforming challenges into rich life experiences.

The book will move, touch and inspire your spirit to face and overcome any of life's adversities. It is a truly inspirational read. Thank you for being the kind open soul you are, John!!"

~ Casey Plouffe, Seven Figure Network Marketer.

"A must-read for anyone facing major changes or challenges in life right now. This book will give you the courage to move through any struggle with confidence, grace, and ease."

~ Jo-Anne Irwin - Transformational Coach and Best Selling Author.

"I have enjoyed the Journey of Riches book series. Each person's story is written from the heart, and everyone's journey is different. We all have a story to tell, and John Spender does an amazing job of finding authors, and combining their stories into uplifting books."

~ Liz Misner Palmer, Foreign Service Officer.

"A timely read as I'm facing a few challenges right now. I like the various insights from the different authors. This book will inspire you to move through any challenge or change that you are experiencing."

~ David Ostrand, Business Owner.

"I've known John Spender for a while now, and I was blessed with an opportunity to be in book four in the series. I know that you will enjoy this new journey like the rest of the books in the series. The collection of stories will assist you with making changes, dealing with challenges, and seeing that transformation is possible for your life."

~ Charlie O' Shea, Entrepreneur.

"A Journey of Riches series will draw you in and help you dig deep into your soul. Authors have unbelievable life stories of purpose inside of them. John Spender is dedicated to bringing peace, love, and adventure to the world of his readers! Dive into this series, and you will be transformed!"

~ Jeana Matichak, Author of Finding Peace.

"Awesome! Truly inspirational! It is amazing what the human spirit can achieve and overcome! Highly recommended!!"

~ Fabrice Beliard, Australian Business Coach and Best Selling Author.

"A Journey of Riches Series is a must-read. It is an empowering collection of inspirational and moving stories full of courage, strength, and heart. Bringing peace and awareness to those lucky enough to read to assist and inspire them on their life journey."

~ Gemma Castiglia, Avalon Healing, Best Selling Author.

"The A Journey of Riches book series is an inspirational collection of books that will empower you to take on any challenge or change in life."

~ Kay Newton, Midlife Stress Buster, and Best Selling Author.

"A Journey of Riches book series is an inspiring collection of stories, sharing many different ideas and perspectives on how to overcome challenges, deal with change and to make empowering choices in your life. Open the book anywhere and let your mood choose where you need to read. Buy one of the books today; you'll be glad that you did!"

~ Trish Rock, Modern Day Intuitive, Bestselling Author, Speaker, Psychic & Holistic Coach.

"A Journey of Riches is another inspiring read. The authors are from all over the world, and each has a unique perspective to share, that will have you thinking differently about your current circumstances in life. An insightful read!"

~ Alexandria Calamel, Success Coach and Best Selling Author.

"The A Journey of Riches book series is a collection of real-life stories, which are truly inspiring and give you the confidence that no matter what you are dealing with in your life, there is a light at the end of the tunnel, and a very bright one at that. Totally empowering!"

~ John Abbott, Freedom Entrepreneur.

"An amazing collection of true stories from individuals who have overcome great changes and who have transformed their lives and used their experience to uplift, inspire and support others."

~ Carol Williams, Author-Speaker-Coach.

"You can empower yourself from the power within this book that can help awaken the sleeping giant within you. John has a purpose in life to bring inspiring people together to share their wisdom for the benefit of all who venture deep into this book series. If you are looking for inspiration to be someone special, this book can be your guide."

~ Bill Bilwani, Renowned Melbourne Restaurateur.

"In the A Journey Of Riches series, you will catch the impulse to step up, reconsider and settle for only the very best for yourself and those around you. Penned from the heart and with an unflinching drive to make a difference for the good of all, A Journey Of Riches series is a must-read."

~ Steve Coleman, author of Decisions, Decisions! How to Make the Right One Every Time.

"Do you want to be on top of your game? A Journey of Riches is a must-read with breakthrough insights that will help you do just that!"

~ Christopher Chen, Entrepreneur.

"In A Journey of Riches, you will find the insight, resources, and tools you need to transform your life. By reading the author's stories, you, too, can be inspired to achieve your greatest accomplishments and what is truly possible for you. Reading this book activates your true potential for transforming your life way beyond what you think is possible. Read it and learn how you, too, can have a magical life."

~ Elaine Mc Guinness, Bestselling Author of Unleash Your Authentic Self!

"If you are looking for an inspiring read, look no further than the A Journey Of Riches book series. The books are an inspiring collection of short stories that will encourage you to embrace life even more. I highly recommend you read one of the books today!"

~ Kara Dono, Doula, Healer and Best Selling Author.

"A Journey of Riches series is a must-read for anyone seeking to enrich their own lives and gain wisdom through the wonderful stories of personal empowerment & triumphs over life's challenges. I've given several copies to my family, friends, and clients to inspire and support them to step into their greatness. I highly recommend that you read these books, savoring the many 'aha's' and tools you will discover inside."

~ Michele Cempaka, Hypnotherapist, Shaman, Transformational Coach & Reiki Master.

"If you are looking for an inspirational read, look no further than the A Journey Of Riches book series. The books are an inspiring and educational collection of short stories from the author's soul that will encourage you to embrace life even more. I've even given them to my clients too so that their journeys inspire them in life for wealth, health and everything else in between. I recommend you make it a priority to read one of the books today!"

~ Goro Gupta, Chief Education Officer, Mortgage Terminator, Property Mentor.

"The A Journey Of Riches book series is filled with real-life short stories of heartfelt tribulations turned into uplifting, self-transformation by the power of the human spirit to overcome adversity. The journeys captured in these books will encourage you to embrace life in a whole new way. I highly recommend reading this inspiring anthology series."

~ Chris Drabenstott, Best Selling Author, and Editor.

"There is so much motivational power in the A Journey of Riches series!! Each book is a compilation of inspiring, real-life stories by several different authors, which makes the journey feel more relatable and success more attainable. If you are looking for something to move you forward, you'll find it in one (or all) of these books."

~ Cary MacArthur, Personal Empowerment Coach

"I've been fortunate to write with John Spender and now, I call him a friend. A Journey of Riches book series features real stories that have inspired me and will inspire you. John has a passion for finding amazing people from all over the world, giving the series a global perspective on relevant subject matters."

~ Mike Campbell, Fat Guy Diary, LLC

"The A Journey of Riches series is the reflection of beautiful souls who have discovered the fire within. Each story takes you inside the truth of what truly matters in life. While reading these stories, my heart space expanded to understand that our most significant contribution in this lifetime is to give and receive love. May you also feel inspired as you read this book."

~ Katie Neubaum, Author of Transformation Calling.

"A Journey of Riches is an inspiring testament that love and gratitude are the secret ingredients to living a happy and fulfilling life. This series is sure to inspire and bless your life in a big way. Truly an inspirational read that is written and created by real people, sharing real-life stories about the power and courage of the human spirit."

~ Jen Valadez, Emotional Intuitive and
Best Selling Author

Table of Contents

Preface

I collated this book and chose the various authors to share their experiences about how they deal with fear. The eclectic collection of chapters encompass a myriad of different writing styles and perspectives that demonstrate what is possible when we take action and confront our deepest darkest fears.

Like all of us, each author has a unique story and insight to share with you. It might so happen that one or more authors have lived through an experience similar to circumstances in your life. Their words could be just the words you need to read to help you through your challenges and motivate you to continue on your chosen path.

Storytelling has been the way humankind has communicated ideas and learning throughout our civilization. While we have become more sophisticated with technology and living in the modern world is more convenient, there is still much discontent and dissatisfaction. Many people have also moved away from reading books, and they are missing valuable information that can help them move forward in life with a positive outlook. Moving towards the tasks or dreams that scare us breeds confidence growing towards becoming better versions of ourselves.

I think it is essential to turn off the T.V.; to slow down and to read, reflect, and take the time to appreciate everything you have in life. Start with an anthology book as they offer a cornucopia of viewpoints relating to a particular theme. In this case, it's fear and how others have dealt with it. I think the reason why we feel stuck in life or having challenges in a particular area is that we see the problem through the same lens that created it. With this compendium and all of the books in the A Journey of Riches series, you have many different writing styles and perspectives that will help you think and see your challenges differently, motivating you to elevate your set of circumstances.

Anthology books are also great because you can start from any chapter and gain valuable insight or a nugget of wisdom without the feeling that you have missed something from the earlier episodes.

I love reading many different types of personal development books because learning and personal growth are vital. If you are not learning and growing, well, you're staying the same. Everything in the universe is growing, expanding, and changing. If we are not open to different ideas and a multitude of ways to think and be, then even the most skilled and educated among us can become close-minded.

The concept of this book series is to open you up to diverse ways of perceiving your reality. It is to encourage you and give you many avenues of thinking about the same subject. My wish for you is to feel empowered to make a decision that will best suit you in moving forward with your life. As Albert Einstein said, "We cannot solve problems with the same level of thinking that created them."

With Einstein's words in mind, let your mood pick a chapter in the book, or read from the beginning to the end and be guided to find the answers you seek.

 If you feel inspired, we would love an honest review on Amazon. This will help create awareness around this fantastic series of books.

With gratitude,
John Spender

"Miracles start to happen when you give as much energy to your dreams as you do to your fears."

~ Richard Wilkins

CHAPTER ONE

---◆---

Overcome The Fear Of Lack
With Abundance Consciousness

By John Spender

You are abundant!

Best write that down, ingrain that into your memory, embrace this truth into your soul. For it is the shield that will protect you from the memes that tell you there isn't enough. The fear of lack is passed down from generation to generation around the world. So many people constantly worry about how they are going to pay the rent. Where is the money going to come from? They ask themselves questions like Why can't I get a better job? Why can't I earn more money? Why can't I be successful? Why can't I get ahead? Why am I always broke? These disempowering questions only reinforce the lack paradigm that most of us find ourselves in at one point in time. But do we really want the solution? Are we desperate to do something about it? Do we want to break the paradigm of lack, limitation, and poverty that has plagued many of our families for centuries?

Who wouldn't say yes, right? Over the following pages, I will share with you principles that I have learned which have guided me to live life abundantly. And if you apply them, you will get the same result as surely as the night turns into day. Maybe you already have a lot of money, but you don't feel like you have enough or fear losing it. Both are part of the same hamburger; they are at opposite ends but are still one and the same. One of the greatest fears of humanity is the fear of lack or of not being enough.

Let's start by spreading abundance consciousness throughout your being like wildfire, a fire that will banish fear, lack, and want from your life. This consciousness is the source of all success, wealth, empowerment, and material gain. The abundance consciousness will draw all to you: a new phone, career, partner, whatever your heart desires. Your wish is your command when connected to this invisible substance that connects all who cultivate its presence. It is omnipresent and so powerful, magnetizing everything in your life to vibrate in harmony with it, dispelling every unwanted condition. If you are lost in a maze of false beliefs, this idea will elevate your experience. If you are in the poor zone, it will take you out. If you are financially down on your luck, it will reach down and pick you up. If you have reached rock bottom, it will take you to the top. If your faith is weak, it will fortify your resolve.

If your attitude is aligned, it will accomplish all things through you. It will amplify the great, increase income, bring riches, activate good, attract opportunities, cancel debts, stimulate business, prevent failure, nourish your aspiration, clarify vision, generate peace, heal wounds, solve problems, expand imagination, return loses, eliminate hardship, remove blocks, dispel fear, squash worry, shut down doubt, integrate the mind, purify judgment, loosen tensions, and open doors. This energy is your Aladdin's lamp to infinite abundance in every area of your life.

You are abundant. Many are its slave and only a few are supported by it. Do you agree? To illustrate this idea, the farmer toils the soil, but the abundant let it work for them. One supports it. The other is supported by it. Is there anyone who puts his hand up for a tough life? Of course not. Yet many are servants to this idea of abundance while others are served by it.

Thoughts are seeds that come to us from anywhere and everywhere as they float through the air looking for the right mental soil. The right soil is a part of consciousness. Just as a vegetable garden must be free from weeds for the garden to thrive, likewise our minds need to be free from negativity, opposing contradictory thoughts, and limiting beliefs if we are to succeed in connecting with abundance consciousness and in becoming abundance itself. The problem is not with the seed, but with the soil. You must remove the impediments of fear, worry, and doubt, and then the idea of abundance can take root and grow to maturity. The unseen becomes seen, starting from nothingness and growing to the manifested. Therefore cultivating the soil of the heart, mind, and soul takes us from an existence of lack and moves us into the fertile grounds of prosperity and abundance.

Firstly, do you know what you desire? Do you know what you deserve? A new apartment? More money or better health? Well, plant your idea into the fertile medium of the subconscious. Plant it deep and cultivate it with recognition and belief, fertilize it with focus and concentration, nurture it with faith and appreciation, all while activating it with your consciousness. If you will only condition your beingness, there is nothing that you can't bring into existence.

You are the universe and the universe is you. When you enter the consciousness of the universe, connecting with its intelligence, you are effectively tapping into all that is and ever was created. The channeler Esther Hicks communicates this through the entity Abraham using the term to enter the vortex of creation. Jesus calls it the Kingdom of Heaven. Suppose we abide in this abundance consciousness and share this quality of consciousness, keeping our thoughts pure and our beingness true to its frequency. Simply allow the divine substance to momentarily shape itself around our thoughts as they materialize into our lives those things which we think and focus on. Moreover, we must keep our minds off our troubles and keep them centered in the universal intelligence that is pure consciousness—abundance consciousness.

Now repeat the affirmation: I am abundance. Say the words with emotion and feel them from your heart. Stake your claim and know your worth. Think abundance throughout the day, for that in which you honor will be honored. Think abundance all the time and watch it manifest in your life in all its various forms. You may be wondering, How I can think of abundance all the time? You do it by making it the primary foundation from which all other words stem. Ralph Waldo Emerson said, "Man is what he thinks about all day long." See abundance in the flowers and the rows of stacked shelves filled with endless goods. See it in the night sky with the bountiful stars shining bright. Feel it in nature through magnificent trees. At any given moment, we are surrounded by abundance. Can you see it?

The character of your main point of focus will be determined by the primary or subjective habit of your thinking. The pattern is the matrix or the fixed mold by which all other thoughts pass. Worry usually starts as a small fear in mind and becomes basic or habitual through repetition. We repeat the same worry day after day until it becomes a habit or an automatic expression. Patterns make a channel or a path through which our thoughts and deeds travel. The channel enlarges as the idea is repeated, getting deeper and wider until the habit tends to influence all our thoughts, actions, and beingness. This is why we are what we think about all day long. If someone's basic thought foundation is worry, everything in her life will be tainted by the specter of anxiety, fear, lack of courage, indecisiveness, coyness, and lack of confidence.

The primary thought is much like a chili paste that Indonesians add to their food, adding heat to everything they eat. Here is a person who has allowed the basic worry thought to permeate his consciousness. The basic worry thought will affect everything in this person's life, spicing all other thoughts with worry. The whole spectrum of negative emotions will stick to it like flies to flypaper. Others will sense the pessimistic mental atmosphere and will be repelled by it. No matter how good or how desirable one's products or services may be, as long as he carries this frequency with him, he will repel his goodness instead of attracting it.

You've heard about the atmosphere of homes, restaurants, buildings, towns, and communities being made up of the collective consciousness of the people who live there. A man's consciousness is related directly to his thoughts, beliefs, and habits—often subtly seeping out in the things he says and does—that reveal him to others. If his basic thought is poverty or lack, others will know it and treat him accordingly.

How then should we approach and change these established habits of thinking? By choosing to embrace a magnanimous beingness towards all life, beginning with adapting new basic thoughts, we will allow those thoughts to crystallize into more productive convictions. Let the same man fill his consciousness with thoughts of assurances, poise, faith, self-confidence, serenity, and inner determination. Let him surround himself with an atmosphere of success, achievement, and strength of character. Let him radiate qualities of fearlessness, inner peace, trust, optimism, and self-reliance. He will attract the best from everything and everybody. He will inspire confidence and compel attention. Believing in himself, he will inspire confidence in others. The new pattern will release universal intelligence into consciousness and change his life's color, character, and tone. Instead of worry, he will generate faith.

This is perhaps the greatest fear that one can indeed face and overcome. The question is, how do you stop yourself from slipping into the primary thought of worry? You do so by tuning the old habit completely out and deliberately and persistently taking a new pattern of confidence and appreciation into your consciousness. The nature of habit is an interesting one moving along the lines of least resistance. This is highlighted clearly by Edward E Beals in his book The Law of Financial Success when he states, "If you have to walk over a field or through a forest you know how natural it is for you to choose the clearest path in preference to the less worn one. And greatly in preference to stepping out across the field or through the woods to form a new path." The line of mental action is precisely the same: movement along the lines of least resistance, passage over the well-worn path.

Patterns are formed through repetition and are developed in accordance with an observable natural law in all animate, and some would say inanimate, things as well. Once paper is folded a particular way, it will fold along the same lines next time. Nature is the best example of this, and notice how rivers and streams of water cut their courses through the land and therefore flow along effortlessly. The law of least resistance is in action everywhere.

The way to eradicate the old process of worry is to form a bigger concept of confidence. As a confident thought grows, the mental path of worry will gradually fill up from disuse. The old path will grow less and less distinct until it eventually disappears. Do you see why this subject is so essential to expanding your abundant consciousness? When you know how to change basic thought, you know how to change everything in your life and are well on the way to something better and more aligned to the consciousness of universal intelligence.

In the initial phase of changing habits, allow patience, persistence, and trust to be your guiding light. The stars don't disappear in daylight hours. They merely disappear from one's sight, but they are still there shining bright as in the night. You will see results when your new conscious credo becomes deeper and stronger than the old unconscious ones. Once the new pattern is outlined and adopted, it must be repeated again and again with immense certainty and feeling for it to take hold. You must make it the intimate and vital predominating ever-living quality of your being, immersing your consciousness in the new paradigm.

Say it to yourself: I am confidence. I am abundance. I am gratitude. I am success. Feel what you say—feel it deeply with all your heart and with great joy. Dwell on your statements until they are firmly synchronized with your emotional nervous system. There are serval rules that will aid you in your embodiment of this new concept of thought and beingness.

1. Refuse to use the old-habit path under any circumstances.
2. Keep your thought changed out of the negative path and hold it positive. If you slip, come back to your new affirmation: I am abundance.
3. Charge the new thought-action with hope, power, belief, conviction, and determination when you express it.

4. Make your new pattern as clear, strong, profound, and as positive as you can.
5. Create opportunities for traveling over this new path as often as possible.

The objective we want to accomplish is two-fold: to annihilate the offending thought pattern of fear and to drop a new idea into the pool of subconscious cerebration so that the new unhindered thought can take form in the creative substance/abundance consciousness. It is a process much like dropping a key or another metal object into a pure body of saltwater. If you have spent time by the ocean, you could conduct this experiment yourself. If you drop a metal key into the water, after a time the water will form itself in a perfect pattern around the key as crystallization. The white layer of salt that covers the key is our new idea forming in our consciousness, over time the salt will erode away the key representing our limiting beliefs and old states of consciousness. We must submerge our consciousness through repetition in our new paradigm. Consciously or unconsciously, you must have a mental equivalent or pattern of the thing desired and, in this case, it is abundance in all its forms. The law of abundance is already within our hearts, subtly pressing the mind to act. Our job is to release it for our daily needs, to open channels for its expression.

Let us think first about the mental analogue or equivalent in this process. This is just another term for basic thought, pattern, or model. Having explored and rid ourselves of all the apparent oppositions, we are now ready to integrate a new model of the subconscious mind's creative forces. We are now ready to drop the key into the water, so to speak.

"Whoever believes in me, as Scripture has said, rivers of living water will flow from within them." (John 7:38) Naturally, the intention is to get the new idea into the soul or subconscious mind. The law does not work for the thing desired while you are forcing it into the conscious mind. It works for fulfillment only when the idea holds you. Therefore the seeds of creation must be planted in the fertile grounds of the subconscious to sprout, take root, and prosper. Let the idea form a consciousness of itself inside you.

Don't hold the idea, but let the idea hold you! Do you feel me? This is crucial to your success. Do not affirm unless the corresponding emotion supports your affirmation. This is where many people come unstuck, as they don't understand this principle. We display our good by first connecting with the universe's intelligence and not through parroting affirmations or mouthing declarations without feeling. The law of attraction responds to us by correlating to our states of mind and our hearts' essence. It operates through our mental equivalent or beliefs. If your heart isn't in it, you are not connected with source. When the principle of abundance is set in motion through affirmation and acceptance, the law of attraction operates through us.

Why must the new thought pattern be housed in the present tense? Why do we say I am abundance instead of saying I will be abundant? Why must we state something we do not have? Life always works in the present moment by direct affirmation. To say I will be abundant is all well and good, but we are putting our abundance off until some future time. To affirm our good in the present is to cause it to appear. Law plus acceptance plus belief is the pattern. If the idea for abundance is to become a superpower in our lives, we must inwardly accept it as a present fact. Our thought, will, and imagination must agree with what we say. We must banish all fear from our being.

Now I'm going to ask you to start building your basic thought pattern for abundance without further delay. Center your thought again in our affirmation I am abundance. This is the nucleus that is to grow and multiply indefinitely. It must be backed up with your persistent faith and desire. Your idea of abundance might be a better position, more income, a nice holiday, a compatible partner, or increased health. The law of attraction says you can have anything you desire, and if you believe you already have it—that is, if you have the objective acceptance of the thing desired.

Now contemplate that for a few moments. Not the money to meet the mortgage, not the new car, not the new house... but the basic idea I *am* abundance. You're going to change your conscious out of the old mold of lack and into the new paradigm of plenty. You're going to create a new habit atmosphere, a new thought inclination, and a new state of beingness. That is your significant responsibility. In the process, you're going to eradicate the mental equivalent of lack by switching to a spiritual equivalent of plenty. You're going to start this idea of abundance revolving on its axis at such an elevated rate of

11

speed that it will draw into your life all the good things you need. You are going to boost your consciousness.

Now put the book down, close your eyes, relax and repeat the affirmation slowly and with purpose one hundred times. Take it easy and feel your pattern deeply, realizing that with each repetition your new idea is going further and further into your subconscious until it is perfectly integrated with your being. It now has the power to attract to it all of the elements that it needs for its fulfillment.

The rest of the process is a matter of sustained attention, faith, feeling, acting, and seeing. See the new idea clearly, realize it, feel it, and accept it. Speed it up with your belief, keep it alive with your faith, feed it with fresh, rich, powerful life-giving images. Give it motion through action, act it out: I am abundance. Discover how rich you are. Keep the abundance idea circulating freely through your mind. See it generating prosperity, opportunities, and success. Do not allow negative ideas to creep in and sabotage your divine good. I am abundance. Keep repeating it until it goes underground and takes form. I am abundance. Feel it's frequency. Rejoice in it. Bless it. Love it. Accelerate the rate of vibration by telling your subconscious mind that you are already abundant.

If you desire abundance, don't say I want to get rid of poverty; be affirmative and positive. Say what you mean, and mean what you say. If your thought is filled with the idea of getting rid of lack, you are increasing lack in your consciousness. Make your primary thought one of prosperity, opulence, plenty, and wealth. Think and speak of nothing else. Oh, yes, I know the rent is due and you have a lot of unpaid bills, but you are not going to think of these right now. You are going to think abundance, know abundance, feel abundance and nothing else. You're going to etch abundance so deeply into your consciousness that nothing else can come into your life. That is what we mean by building a new mental equivalent. It's creating a new basic thought out of impulsion that will flood your life with good. It is making a new path for God by getting everything out of her way. It takes everything out of your consciousness that is unlike perfection and trading it in for something better and more desirable. The issue is not with life, but with the use that you are making of it. If you change your condition from poverty to abundance, you must change your position with the law of attraction.

Seven-Day Action Plan

So are you ready for practical application? Here's what I want you to do for the next seven days: I want you to work with purpose, deliberation, and persistence on this one idea. I am abundance. I want you to think of nothing else and feel nothing else for this period. This doesn't mean that you will get your manifestation in seven days, although it could happen right now. I want you to watch your attitude, thought, feeling, and conversation during that period of time to see that you never revert to your old way of thinking and feeling. Know what you desire and declare it with such a convincing tone that the subconscious will go right to work to materialize your aspiration. Expect miracles.

Now let us repeat your seven-day action plan for this week beginning right now. You are going to take the idea I am abundance and think of nothing else for seven days. If negative or contradictive thoughts sneak in, catch yourself and refuse to entertain or give them any energy by coming back to your idea. If that sinus issue or arthritis starts to bother you, if the job becomes stressful, if debt or the housing problem presses, you reject the thought. Say, I'm not going to talk about illness, the job, those unpaid bills, and the apartment. I'm going to only think about wealth and health. I am abundance. This is your new thought pattern and habit for your life. It is the basic thought by which we test every other thought. You shall weave it so tightly into the fabric of your consciousness that no threat of the old process of poverty can find room.

I am abundance. Say it over and over, think of it, dream it, make it the intimate powerful and ever-loving quality of your beingness. Say it to yourself. I am abundance. I am prosperity. I am affluence. I am wealthy. I am successful. Feel these new patterns. Feel them deeply, intensely, with a sense of determination. Feel them incessantly. Thank God for them. Celebrate their goodness, and let them sink innately into your nervous system.

If you are serious about changing the automatic expression of your life and leaving your past conditioning behind, I want to give you a little suggestion that will help you. I have found this association method to be beneficial, and I'm sure you will, too. Take any object that you handle many times a day like your phone, water bottle, pen, toothbrush, razor, or keys and every time you pick them up, say, I am thinking of abundance, I am thinking of plenty, I am thinking of prosperity. When you turn the key in the ignition of your car a dozen or so times a day, use that act as an association opportunity to expand and ingrain your idea deeper into your consciousness. Let it remind you that you are abundant. Accept the reminder when you unlock the door of your home, when you open the fridge, when you turn on the computer, when you check your social media, when you spend money, when you get dressed, when you tie your shoes, when you wash dishes, when you clean and tidy the house. If you do this insightfully and systematically for even seven days, you'll be amazed at the beneficial change and blessings that will come into your life.

What Abundance Is

Few things are more sought after or more misunderstood than what the average person calls abundance. To a shop assistant, a raise of $50 a week is abundant, while to a wizard on Wall Street, a profit of a million dollars is abundance. This great difference in perspective is because the value in which abundance is defined is false. Abundance is not a matter of money. Ask any number of people you meet to define their ideas of abundance, and you'll most likely get a hundred different answers. What does this prove? It shows that plenty is a state of well-being. It implies a free and easy access to all that is good and desirable. Wealth comes by the same law that metal filings come to a steel magnet. The power of attraction is not in the bar of steel, but in the invisible force with which it is charged. So it is with supply. It comes not by hard work, physical effort, or will power, but by infinite intelligence, a form of consciousness—abundance consciousness—a Divine Grand Order Design—or, if you like, God. This infinite intelligence is embodied as a working force in consciousness. This power draws material riches to one in abundant measure. These riches come not because of anything that a person does on the outer plane, but by virtue of her consciousness or by his beingness.

We instinctively sense those things are true, but we don't always know how to become receptive. When we get into a state of lack or want, it's so real to us that we can't think of anything else. Our static or undisciplined thought perpetuates lack. Everything we need or desire is at hand, but we must resolve it into what we require. How do we transform the invisible substance into visible wealth? By the cultivation and the circulation of rich ideas. When we identify ourselves with rich ideas, ideas of wealth, opulence, affluence, prosperity, and plenty, we become channels fit to receive the outpouring of God's abundance. In other words, we must shape our thoughts, desires, and aspirations to the divine pattern. Since abundance is in the divine plan for us, it is our duty to express prosperity in every phase of our living. Since it is our divine right to be abundant and successful, there must lie hidden in the soul the possibility of a greater experience. This infinite possibility will remain inactive until we set it into motion.

If we have been in the habit of thinking of abundance in terms of money or material possessions, we must change our thought. True abundance is reflected with one's connection to universal intelligence. It is not an end in itself, but a means to greater freedom, increased livingness, and a fuller expression of life. It is related not by the number of things that a person owns but to the satisfaction that a person finds in them, how a person uses them, and the happiness derived from them. True abundance is not measured in terms of palaces, servants, cars, chauffeurs, fur coats, and real estate. True abundance is measured in connection with source, contentment, confidence, freedom, inspiration, beauty, and a clear conscience. It is measured by abounding health and energy, rich thoughts, deep awareness, and humorous relations with others. It is measured by love and devotion of friends, guidance in times of uncertainty, courage in the presence of fear, protection from danger, peace of mind, and a sense of joy at realizing that you are the universe and its unlimited supply.

If we are honest with ourselves, we have to admit that our chief concern has not always been in deep connection with the universe, but with the things of the world. This is due in a large part to our social conditioning that money is everything.

Money is a manifestation of substance. Substance is an attribute of divine mind. To gain an adequate comprehension of the omnipresence of substance is to acknowledge the source of creation as our soul/sole provider. If we are not manifesting as we would desire, this is a warning that we should turn the force of our thought towards consciousness and its infinite riches.

The dictionary defines abundance as a very large quantity of something, the state or condition of having a copious quantity of something; plentifulness. To be abundant in this sense is to have access to everything where and when it's needed. It would enable one to face the future with a confidence in the knowledge that whatever she needed would always be present when any need might appear. There is any number of reasons why we suffer from lack. Knowing that you deserve abundance is a trusted guiding principle that never fails. Many people go wrong because they ask for too little and settle for less than they deserve. A person fails to ask for the best because of his or her own limiting beliefs.

What we need is a more extensive awareness of the universal intelligence, inexhaustible substance, and a capacity for acceptance aligned with our claim. Our desires must be definite and flexible, and we should always expect something better than the thing we have set our hearts on. The purpose of our desires is to open our consciousness so that we can use the expanded form, enlarging our connection to Source. See it as a process of evolving your consciousness. It is the nature of abundance consciousness to out do itself. The gift is to attain a new state of expansion. When we start to connect with this higher consciousness, we clear the invisible channels to become visible. When our abundance is the outward growth of a rich consciousness, it is satisfying, permanent, and secure. Our job is to raise our vibration and feel worthy enough to receive, thereby creating a new state of beingness.

Ten Points To Cultivate And Increase Your Abundance Consciousness

1. The mental process necessary to draw a greater income is a matter of recognition, connection, acceptance, appreciation, and belief. This spiritual experience must precede any material manifestation.

2. Supply is fundamentally an invisible thing. It is the receiving into your consciousness through an intimate relationship with Source, the creator of all things from the beginning and out of which all things are formed.

3. The metaphysical method for demonstrating abundance is to put abundant ideas to work.

4. Poverty is a state of mind. We bring about this manifestation by our negative recognition, past conditioning, acceptance and beliefs. The fear of lack creates more lack, period.

5. We overcome poverty by mastering our point of focus. Remember: what we focus on expands and is what we eventually become. It's an exercise of substituting lack with abundant consciousness and requires much the same discipline as physical exercise.

6. We look not to the things, persons, and places for solving a supply problem; we solve this by looking within our own consciousness.

7. We master the sense of want by building an inner sense of plenty.

8. We can have anything we desire if we believe that we already have it and embrace that belief with a sense of gratitude.

9. Abundance is not a matter of education, training, working, saving and investing, struggling, or denying yourself. It's a matter of getting into harmony with your own individual consciousness and then following the law to its logical conclusion.

10. The permanent source of our abundance lies within our power to possess and mold universal divine substance within our thoughts.

The value of repetition cannot be emphasized enough. It's like the constant dropping of water on a stone leaving its mark. It is the continuous repetition of your affirmation that fuses it with the subconscious mind and therefore materializes the idea.

In conclusion, I would like to thank you for spending the last 15-20 minutes with me and I encourage you to reread this chapter as many times as needed. I recommend that you seek the more rooted blessings found in abundant living, as well as the gratification it brings to such a worthwhile endeavor. God bless you, my friend, as you depend on abundance consciousness for all you will ever need, and abundance consciousness never ceases to deliver.

**"Running away from your problems
is a race you will never win."**

~ Bruce Van Horn

CHAPTER TWO

---◆---

Staying True To Myself By Overcoming Fear

By Dr. Colleen Sabol-Olitsky

"All men are driven by faith or fear—one or the other—for both are the same. Faith or fear is the expectation of an event that hasn't come to pass or the belief in something that cannot be seen or touched. A man of fear always lives on the edge of insanity. A man of faith lives in perpetual reward."

- Andy Andrews, *The Traveler's Gift: Seven Decisions that Determine Personal Success*

Does The Idea Of A Career Change Sound As Scary As Hell?

D o you remember your earliest memories of what you wanted to be when you grew up? I can vividly recall being in middle school and playing at recess with my friend, also named Colleen. We played the game MASH and discussed the future and what we wanted it to look like. We wrote down the boys we liked, the states we wanted to live in, the cars we wanted to drive, and the careers we'd like to pursue. I always picked states like Florida, California, and Hawaii. For my job, I would add an artist or gym teacher to the list, but deep down, I knew that I wanted to be a doctor, so of course, that was always included on my list. Both Colleen and I had crushes on boys named Brian (two different boys) and we would squeal with laughter as the pencil circled the lists of wants and desires and landed on the things we truly wanted.

Fast forward thirty-five years, and I found myself sitting in the dental office, Smile Stylist, that I had built with my husband. I had done it! I pursued my dream of being a doctor and had chosen dentistry and married my dental school sweetheart, Jason, and we lived in Florida with our two kids, then three and six. Everything I had ever wanted came true and I was living my dream life, or so it seemed from the outside. But the truth was, I was miserable.

"Comparison is the thief of joy."

~ Teddy Roosevelt

Comparing yourself to others is an awful way to waste your energy and talents. I loved being a dentist the first few years out of school. I loved the communication and building relationships by helping patients to understand their options. We were doing everything we could so that they would have a good experience instead of the all-too-common "I hate the dentist."

But as time went on, Jason began to grow into an incredible cosmetic dentist. He always had good hands and was very artistic, even in school. I had been adequate in those areas. I could study and ace a test, but I couldn't make my fillings look as pretty as Jason's. And this would ultimately be the start of how I lost my passion for dentistry.

After working for a corporate dental office for a few years, we opened our own practice and Jason continued to hone his expertise. I continued to lose more and more confidence, in both myself and my abilities. The truth is—and I can see it now—I was a good dentist. I got the job done, my patients liked me, and it was fine. But I couldn't let go of the fact that Jason had skyrocketed to success within the profession for his passion and mastery for smile makeovers. I felt left behind, not good enough. These emotions left me feeling angry, resentful, and full of shame. I couldn't tell anyone how I felt because that would be admitting that I was a failure, and that scared me to death.

Growing up in a house full of criticism and judgment, I never felt good enough. When I brought home a B, I was grilled on why I didn't get an A. When I chose a certain pair of shoes for my dental school graduation, I was teased for having poor taste and asked why I chose those. Basically, I would zig and get questioned for why I didn't zag. I had to explain, defend, and justify myself continually. And for most of my life, I was able to grit my teeth and push through to succeed at whatever I was doing, using that anger to fuel and push me.

But I was quickly losing ground here; I simply couldn't bury these feelings of inadequacy anymore. How could I face my fears about not being good enough? I would wonder, should I stick with dentistry and try to make it work, or should I just quit? Would that make me a quitter? A failure? How could I possibly explain that to my family? These are the negative thoughts that haunted me for years.

How Do You Admit To Yourself And Those Around You That You Are Not Happy?

As I've mentioned, I had enjoyed dentistry in my early years, but as time went on, I felt less and less excited about it and more and more stressed. We all know that, once your heart is no longer in something, you begin to dread every day, and I began to feel a hefty dose of resentment towards the office and the overall profession.

I knew that I needed a change, but how? You can't just walk away from something that you are so heavily invested in after all of this time, money and effort. I had a hard time confiding my feelings to anyone because I felt guilty for lacking gratitude and happiness for all of the blessings I had in my life. But, also, I wondered what else I was going to do. I had spent eight years and two hundred thousand dollars to become a dentist and over seven hundred thousand to build out our dental office; I couldn't just stop being a dentist.

The fear of the unknown can also be daunting, especially to those who have spent their entire careers in a specific area, and particularly in medicine because of the huge investment and sacrifice that is required. Just the thought of walking away filled me with more fear than relief. I was afraid to share my feelings with anyone, including my family, friends, and colleagues. I had so many conversations in my head about what I should say, how I would say it, and imagining everyone's reactions to how I was feeling. My thoughts would just spiral and leave me feeling trapped.

I was good at hiding my despair and did so for years, but as time passed, I could feel it growing. After an intense few months of holding them in, I finally confessed my feelings of unhappiness and anger to my husband, who received it better than I thought he would. Looking back, I'm sure he sensed my sadness. It helped to talk about it, but I still felt I'd be disappointing so many people, especially my parents.

The whole thing brought me back to a memory that will always stick in my mind. It was the end of my sophomore year of college when I met with my advisor and we sat down to catch up and discuss my future. I said that I wanted to go to medical school, and I still remember how he laughed and said simply that that was not possible, not with a 2.5 GPA.

I was stunned. I had always been able to work for what I wanted and make it happen. I didn't like being told no or that I couldn't do something. I left that meeting and went home to talk to my parents.

When I told them about my meeting, my mom was not happy. She asked, "What are you going to do?" All I could think of was to be a science teacher, maybe? I had never thought about doing or being anything else besides some sort of doctor. But the reality was that I had no medical professional role models or mentors. I had no one to give me advice on what I should've been doing. I'd thought that getting decent grades at a tough school was just as good as getting better grades at a more relaxed school.

I could tell that my mom was so disappointed. Despite a grant and student loan I had gotten, my parents had covered the rest of my tuition. And this school was not inexpensive. I knew that I could've been giving a similar effort at a state school for way less money. I knew something had to change.

I made the decision right then and there to clean up my act and make better choices. I also committed to getting straight As for my last two years of school, hopefully giving me a chance to pursue my dream. So here I was, 20 years later, ready to tell my parents that I didn't want to be a dentist anymore. Again, that fear of disappointing two of the people I love the most was almost enough for me to just stick with dentistry, despite knowing that it was time to start looking for a different career path.

Don't Ignore That Annoying Little Voice Inside Of You

Not everyone knows what they want to do early in life, but as I grew older, the desire to be a doctor continued to burn inside of me. I wanted to help people feel better, but I also wanted the prestige and wealth of being a doctor. I worked hard throughout college and, with much introspection, decided that being a medical doctor was not for me. As I had also started thinking about what kind of doctor I wanted to be, I realized how I did not like being in hospitals, and not that anyone likes it, but I could not handle death very well. Having to deliver the devastating news to family members that their loved one had passed made me sick; I just knew I wasn't cut out for that. To this day, I am so grateful that I listened to my intuition and followed what I instinctively knew.

During my junior year of college, I started to think about medical careers that didn't involve death. I thought that maybe physical therapy might be a path for me since I loved sports so much, even playing in a Division 1 field hockey program in college. With that passion in mind, during that first semester, I did an internship at a physical therapy facility and absolutely hated it! I thought it would be all young athletes and training and excitement. Instead, I found it was working with older people who were feeling pretty miserable and just trying to gain back some mobility. I just knew it wasn't for me. Again, I listened to that nagging voice deep inside leading me to a different path.

I asked myself, what was another field in medicine where you weren't responsible for someone's life? Then I thought of how I had been born with two missing permanent teeth and how I loved going to the dentist. During high school, I had to have surgery to expose my canine in the roof of my mouth, put a bracket on it to pull it down into place, and then have two bridges to replace my missing laterals. It was all so fascinating to me. So I called several local dentists and found an older one open to having an intern work with him for free.

I would spend several afternoons a week just learning the basics in an assistant's role and I loved it! That summer, I decided to leave my lifeguarding job to work as an assistant in a large dental practice so that I could gain more experience and learn more about the profession. I knew it was what I had to do, and I was excited, but the thought of being inside all day instead of sitting out by a pool crushed me! I loved being outside and feeling the sunshine on my body. However, I made the best of it by wearing a sports bra under my scrubs and going out for a walk every day during my lunch break. Some days, I would just lie out in the grass under the sun. Although I loved being an assistant, I also dreaded missing my summer days, but I figured it was time to grow up. After all, this is what adults do. This would be a time when I would ignore that little voice inside my head and just do what I thought I was destined to do—be a dentist.

But that crazy thought of being trapped inside all day when the sun was shining bright would also be a huge factor in my decision to leave dentistry.

What Are They Going To Think?

How often do we let the fear of "what will they think" dictate the choices we make in life? I have many conversations today with teammates who let the opinions of others control their happiness and success. I am thrilled that I took a chance and faced my fears so that I can now inspire others to do the same thing—all with a lot of hard work and belief! By the summer of 2014, when I was going to the office instead of spending the summer days with my kids at the pool and beach, I finally just broke. I couldn't do it anymore. I was miserable and I wanted out!

Meanwhile, I had been watching an acquaintance's network marketing journey on Facebook and she seemed so positive and happy. She was helping so many people and earning an incredible income, and she had just posted that she was looking for two new business partners! Ten years prior to all of this, I knew nothing about network marketing (or MLMs, as they used to be called), but I had read about them in several books about creating multiple streams of income and had always been curious. I was so afraid to take that first step of even contacting her because, in doing so, I would not only have to admit to myself how unhappy I was but also, in potentially making this significant change, I would have to confront my parents, family, and colleagues.

I just knew that I would be met with so much resistance. Family members would criticize me, as they were used to me being a people-pleaser and going with the flow, and my dentist friends would be judging me as well. I knew that they wouldn't understand, especially since Jason not only taught other dentists how to perform dental treatments, but he also wanted to inspire and motive them to love what they do. Now, here I was admitting my despair and trying to find a way out. And I was also wrestling with the internal consequences, which can be just as painful as those external ones. If I weren't a dentist and were not building our Smile Stylist brand alongside my husband anymore, who would I be?

Shedding the persona associated with the old me and finding a way to redefine myself felt like a full-blown identity crisis. What I didn't realize is that we consistently underestimate our own resilience. We are far more capable than we give ourselves credit.

One Life, That's All You've Got!

**"Only those who dare to fail
greatly can achieve greatly."**

-Robert F. Kennedy

Despite my hesitation, I think I was just desperate enough and intrigued enough to give my Facebook friend a call. I can remember our conversation. I was on the beach with my family, and to be honest, it wouldn't have mattered what she said; I was in. Despite my doubts about potentially changing careers, I ordered my nutrition package and within six weeks of sharing a few posts on Facebook, I had earned seventeen hundred dollars. Not bad. During that time, I was still working part-time at the office since my youngest was only at school for half-days. I would spend several hours studying network marketing, leverage, and residual income, and I could feel my confidence growing with this new venture. I felt like I had finally found my people.

Everyone was so inspiring and empowering. I wasn't being compared to Jason anymore. I felt like I was able to forge my own path and not be in his shadow. And I loved being able to work from my phone outside in my back yard while my daughter took her afternoon nap. Now, this was more like it!

But not everyone shared my new hopes and happiness. As expected, my parents were not happy that I'd quit dentistry to "sell shakes." My in-laws were appalled with this decision, and my colleagues all thought I was nuts. I spent many hours in my head thinking about how I would be explaining and defending myself to everyone around me. The network marketing industry had such a bad reputation; how could I make others see what I had seen in such a short amount of time?

As I learned more about the network marketing profession, I fell deeper in love with everything it represented and offered. I still loved dentistry, but it just wasn't for me anymore. I think everyone thought that this transition to network marketing was just a phase, perhaps a way to deal with being burnt out, but it's been almost six years now and I just know that this is what I am meant to do. I love helping people with every aspect of their lives: physically, financially, mentally, and spiritually. I earn an incredible income. I get to do it on my terms, meaning that I work my business when and where I want, including outside by the pool and beach! It's truly my dream job!

My family—meaning my husband, parents, and in-laws— have come to accept my choice to leave dentistry behind and pursue my passion. I didn't need their approval, but it sure helps. I still receive plenty of criticism from most dentists when I share what I do now. I am in several dental Facebook groups and they are always asking about ways to earn additional streams of income. Dentistry is demanding, physically and mentally, stressful, and the insurance and overheads are a killer. Even if you love it, that is the reality most dentists face. Having a plan B is smart, especially considering what is happening as I write this. Dental offices across the country were mandated to be closed in March because of COVID-19, and some still are, and it's been nearly three months! How scary financial security can be taken away! I know we were fortunate to experience much less stress during these unprecedented times because my income never stopped, so it was less of a big deal that Jason's did. We are both so grateful that I took a chance and said yes, because it has been life-changing in so many ways!

Over the years, I have learned that our comfort zones can either cause us to expand or to contract. We are told to "lean in" or "just do it." But we tend to thrive through routine and predictability. It gives a sense of control, so when there are big changes, we are suddenly thrown into a state of uncertainty.

A 2016 study found that it's not the potential negative outcomes that stress us out. Instead, it's the inherent ambiguity that lies in not knowing. The less confident we are about what will happen to us, the more scared and miserable we are. The study found that not knowing what's coming causes more stress than knowing, absolutely, that something terrible will happen. When it comes to motivation, uncertainty is the big, nasty culprit behind why we consider staying in a mediocre romantic relationship or at a terrible job for longer periods than we should.

There are so many faces of fear, and I think we are all pretty familiar with most of them, everything from small anxiety to a full-on panic attacks, or from little worries to crippling and chronic ones. But every time we let go of fear and just do the thing, we find that we can lessen those negative feelings.

Is it a true fear or just the fear of uncertainty that keeps us from leaping over to a potentially better place? We wait until the pain is great enough to pivot in a different direction. But is there a way to shift our thinking and take that leap before our situation gets so bad? One thing to ask ourselves is, "What's the worst that can happen?" Most times, we can honestly say that we will not die, nor will the world stop spinning. And from there we can learn to acknowledge and accept the fear, and as we do, we gain the courage to face the situation and boost our self-esteem.

We all have seen how we benefit from liberating ourselves from a fearful situation and how that learning and success spills over into other areas of our lives. It's in this place that we can begin to feel happier and more capable.

"Inaction breeds doubt and fear. Action breeds confidence and courage.

If you want to conquer fear, do not sit home and think about it.

Go out and get busy."

~ Dale Carnegie

Today, I know that I am a different person and I am more capable to responding to both inner and outer conflicts, but I am not perfect. I still sometimes fall victim to the comparison game within my network marketing profession. I ask myself why I am not further along in my business, why haven't I attracted another business builder, or I doubt that consistently being in the top 150 top income earners is good enough and why can't I break through to the top 100 like so and so. But I am quick to catch myself and remind myself that because of my decision to say yes thousands of lives have been impacted, and that is what matters. No amount of money or recognition will ever fulfill my inner void of self-love, so that is where I place my focus. I won't allow my insecurities to ruin what a beautiful life I have created. You too can develop this awareness and strength, but only if you face your fear and take that first step.

In closing, I hope my chapter has left you inspired to take a chance and go do the thing that is holding you back! I had no way of knowing how these last six years were going to turn out, but I am forever grateful that I took a leap of faith and said yes to the unknown. In doing so, I've been able to heal my past, dream about the future, and truly enjoy the present.

**"The cave you fear to enter holds
the treasure that you seek."**

~ Joseph Campbell

CHAPTER THREE

❖

10,000 Feet To 10 Feet

By Tracy Sotirakis

I t was the heart of my busy wedding season and I was working myself to utter exhaustion. As a freelance professional makeup artist and hairstylist, I had to take jobs when they came. I tried not to complain about getting up at two o'clock in the morning to get a bride ready for her sunrise nuptials. It really was terrible, though. It always felt like I had to say yes to every job that came my way or else my bills would not get paid. Work and money were all that mattered during the wedding season, nothing else.

On one particular day, I had two bookings, one at three in the morning and another at seven in the morning. I was already tired from the previous day's job. It was typical for the wedding season, and I set out with the grim determination just to get the job done. But I didn't know that today would be different. Today would change my life.

The first booking went well and I proceeded to the seven o'clock one. When I arrived at my client's hotel room, I was greeted by a cute ten-year-old boy and a friendly lady

39

who introduced herself as Miss Marilyn; she said that's what everybody calls her. The room was a complete disaster and I had barely enough room to set up my makeup supplies. There was a massive amount of cute jewelry scattered everywhere, along with suitcases overflowing with clothing and shoes.

With makeup clients, I always ask them what they want in terms of style. Miss Marilyn told me that she was going to the grand opening party of a new corporate office and that she needed to look very glamorous. She told me the company's name and that she sold jewelry. I thought, "Ok, cool lady, whatever, just sit down so I can do your makeup and then go home and take a nap."

Once we finished, Miss Marilyn's little boy gave me a pair of earrings. She gave me her business card, though she didn't actually try to recruit me. She simply said, "You don't have to be working this hard, honey." A few days later, I woke up very early in the morning with one thought: "I should sell that jewelry too. Why not?" A little spare money in my pocket could really help me out as well. I contacted Miss Marilyn and she was over the moon with excitement for me. We went through the signing up process and I was in. I figured that I had a built-in clientele with my makeup clients and the jewelry was adorable, so I'd do great.

Reality smacked me hard in the face when I started researching how top consultants accomplished sales for this company. It was mostly by doing live videos on Facebook. Live, as in not recorded? Oh crap. What did I get myself into? I didn't want to be on camera! I'm kind of shy! This would also mean that I had to announce this whole new business on my Facebook account, where everybody knew me as a well-established makeup artist. All I could imagine was the impending judgment from every single person that I knew. My colleagues in the TV and photography business would talk behind my back about what a failure I was as a makeup artist. And truth be told, I'd been in a bad situation for years where I was told I could do nothing right. The thought of taking this risk, of putting myself out there in such a personal way, made me feel so terrified that I considered quitting the jewelry business immediately. There was no way that I could do it. I was petrified and felt so stupid for even thinking that I could start selling something like this.

My boyfriend, Eric, was the first one that I told about the new job. He was very supportive and encouraged me to try it out. I began hesitantly telling a few people in my inner circle. As I'd feared, I received some negative reactions, asking me why I would be doing something below me like selling jewelry. Did I even have time for it? What was I thinking? I had a great career as a makeup artist. One person that I told just stared at me with his mouth open. He didn't even say a word. My heart was crushed. I felt so foolish.

Miss Marilyn, fortunately, became my mentor and encouraged me to keep going. She told me that many people would discourage me and even shame me, but if I tried my best, I would make money and thrive. I made my mind up to ignore the haters who didn't believe in me or want to give me any support. Nonetheless, I was still absolutely horrified about doing live jewelry sales on Facebook, to the point where it made me feel sick.

My first live show, I was a nervous wreck. So many bad things can happen on a live show and thinking about them all was terrifying. I procrastinated for a long time but finally got the nerve to do it. My hands were shaking so much that I dropped things. My mouth was dry and I stumbled over my words. The crazy thing was that nobody was even watching me. Not one person. I think that actually made it worse. It made me feel like more of a failure because I had no customers, so of course, I didn't sell anything. What was I thinking of starting a new business that I knew nothing about? It was not going well at all.

Being a makeup artist and working in the television industry, you might think I would be comfortable, or at least less scared, to be on camera. I wasn't. Normally when filming a TV show, or even a commercial ,there is a director to coach and coddle you. A lighting person is making sure that you look good. The wardrobe department picks out nice clothes for you. I had none of that support system. It was only me and my phone camera, set up in the spare bedroom in the basement of our house.

If I wanted my little side business to work, I just had to keep going. I couldn't let the constant fear of judgment and rejection take me over. I worked on changing my mindset. If nobody watched or bought, I would say to myself, "I did my best, next time will be better." I mentioned this to myself multiple times a day, every single day. To my surprise, it did get easier. I began to get more comfortable the more I practiced. Every time I pushed the "Live Video" button, it went more smoothly. The most wonderful thing was that I actually started selling jewelry! That was the only sign that I needed to keep going.

My main reason for looking for a different career was something that I was afraid to admit to anyone, let alone announce it to the world, especially on Facebook. The truth is that I was totally and completely burnt out in my career as a makeup artist, especially for weddings. I was terrified about anybody finding this out, but I had been thinking about it for quite a few years. My clients and colleagues couldn't know – it would spell the end of my job as a makeup artist. My friends and family would think I was nuts. Being a makeup artist for 19 years was my entire identity.

But the two years leading up to starting my jewelry business had been extremely stressful. I live in a rural area, hours away from most of my clients. Spending four to six hours driving a day was long and dangerous; working a full day on top of the hours spent in the car left me completely exhausted. My equipment is heavy and I have to lug it in and out of the car and up and downstairs to different hotels for bridal clients, sometimes several times a day. My back was constantly in pain, my arms would go numb from driving for so long, and I put about 35,000 miles on my car.

Also, a lot of the clients just didn't respect me. Many of them were just downright rude to me for no reason. It felt like they considered me nothing more than a little teenage girl that just wanted to play dress up with them for fun. In reality, I am highly educated and extensively trained in my art. I have done makeup for well-known celebrities, famous politicians, and billionaires. Once, a snotty bridesmaid sat down in my chair to get made up and said to me in a threatening way, "Don't make me look like a clown." It took all of my restraint, not just to pack up my equipment and walk out. Doing what I once absolutely loved had become a chore that I couldn't wait to stop doing. And it didn't help that, for a long time, I had no emotional support at home from my (soon to be) ex-husband – quite the opposite, in fact.

I knew that I had to find another way to make money, but I was so stuck that it scared me to start over. I have no college degree, backup plan, or giant savings account. Being self-employed for so long, there was no way that I could go to work for a traditional boss. I would either get fired or simply be miserable. Where do you start over when you have no plan?

When the jewelry opportunity came up, I was relieved. I was in a healthier relationship and I knew that something had to change. I believed that if I wanted to make it happen, I could do it with hard work, even if it included doing things way out of my comfort zone. Luckily, it did grow with the time that I put in and I enjoyed it more and more. The live sales, which had been an absolute nightmare in the beginning, became something fun that I looked forward to. I had learned a significant amount, and was doing so much better that other consultants started looking up to me. Putting myself out into the world despite the fact that I was scared made me better at it, and other people sure took notice.

In March of 2020, the COVID-19 virus hit us in the United States. We all went on full quarantine in the middle of March. I began to call it "lockdown" because that's how I felt. Around day four of lockdown, it hit me hard emotionally. March is normally the beginning of my busy wedding season for makeup, and despite the inroads I'd made in selling jewelry, my calendar was full of weddings booked for the rest of the year. But once the lockdown started, the cancellations began pouring in. Within a few days, all my work and income as a makeup artist for the rest of the year had vanished. For a freelancer, looking at an empty calendar is the most terrifying thing in the world.

No one in my immediate circle of family and friends seemed to understand how devastating this was for me. I felt completely alone. Most of my older family members were retired and had savings. Other friends and family members just had to transition to working from home or had jobs deemed essential and were still working. And there I was, with nothing. Watching the news in the morning brought me to tears with fear, worry and pity for myself. I was really in deep trouble.

I applied for every kind of small business loan or government assistance right away. The responses that I received were all denials, because I was self-employed. I was attempting to go about my life and keep busy at home, but by the second week of lockdown, I finally just crumbled. I lay on the floor in my office and bawled my eyes out.

Eric tried to console me. I confessed to him how terrified I was that I had just lost my whole business of nineteen years. I had essentially been fired. He rubbed my back for a while then reminded me that I still had my jewelry business. Even through more uncontrollable sobbing, I knew what I needed to do. Work. But would people buy jewelry online during a pandemic? With people everywhere suffering economically, I couldn't imagine that I would be able to sell anything. I turned to my mentor for help. She had never been through a pandemic before, of course, but she knew the jewelry business. Miss Marilyn's advice was to be nothing but purely positive and give my customers something happy and uplifting to watch. They wanted love, positivity, and something enjoyable to take their minds off their own current problems.

I decided to change my live jewelry sales pitches into more of a show. Even though I felt like absolute garbage and was scared out of my mind by my current financial situation, I didn't let any of my online viewers know. I began to think of myself as an actress. With so many people sitting home in their pajamas, I dressed up and always had my hair and makeup done, which gave me more confidence. I beamed utter positivity and love during my shows. And my Facebook family of viewers noticed what I was doing. I began to receive messages daily, thanking me for doing something that made them laugh and feel good. I noticed that it actually made me feel better on the inside too. Acting positive made me feel positive, as cheesy as that sounds.

Needing to expand and do more videos, I was encouraged by my mentor to do something else other than selling jewelry to keep people engaged during these tough times. Staying home, I was doing a ton of cooking and baking, so Eric and I decided to share some of my recipes in our live videos. This again terrified me because I am in no way at all a professional cook or baker. I just like to cook and bake for fun. What scared me so much about our new food videos was the extreme judgment that I could get from viewers. People online can be ruthless if you do the wrong thing, especially with cooking and baking. What if I displayed poor knife skills, used the incorrect terminology, or looked unsanitary? I could only imagine the harsh comments coming my way.

Every cooking show was different, but I usually got through them without something bad happening. Then came the fudge video. I did a show demonstrating how to make my famous chocolate walnut fudge, which I have made a million times for Christmas gifts. I had almost finished demonstrating how to cook the fudge when all of a sudden the fudge that I was stirring in the pan, live on camera with a bunch of people watching, fully seized up from getting too hot. It was totally burnt. With all the chaos of filming and being nervous and trying to do everything perfectly, I didn't know that my stove burner was too high. Of course, I wanted to hide it on camera and ended the video quickly after. I was mortified.

We cleaned up the kitchen and I retreated to my bathroom to take a shower. I was close to tears and beating myself up mentally for burning the fudge. Why was I putting myself through this torture to do stupid live videos and make myself look like a moron in front of the world? I stood with my head under the hot water for a while. I didn't want to go back to reality because I was terrified of what people were going to say about me messing up on the camera. So many possible horrible comments crossed my mind.

Eric came into the bathroom to check on me. He knew that I was distraught. We chatted for a minute then out of nowhere, he laughed and said, "Did you hear me fart during the video?" This completely broke me, but in a good way. I kneeled in the shower and laughed hysterically for a few minutes, letting the tears freely flow. That simple confession made me realize that negative things happen all the time to everyone, not just me, and we have to see the humor in our failures. The fact that I was still putting myself out there and doing all these things that frightened me to the core made me feel incredibly empowered to keep going.

I appreciate my "little side business" every single day because a few years before, I would have never been allowed to do it—yes, allowed. I was married and in an extremely controlling relationship. My husband would have viewed selling jewelry as beneath me and not a real job. He would never have allowed me even to consider doing it.

Our marriage didn't start poorly, but got worse throughout the years. As time went on, the less and less I was permitted to do and the more unhappy I became. My makeup business was something that he controlled tightly, even though he really had very little to do with it. If the pay rate weren't something that he thought was good enough, he would demand that I turn down the job, even though we constantly struggled financially. I would work and drive long hours but still be responsible for cooking and cleaning, though he was home most of the time.

The longer it went on, the longer it felt like my personality, who I was deep inside, was evaporating. The only clothing that I was allowed to purchase was the style and brands approved by him. Anything else was a fight, so I just gave in. He even demanded that I wear certain types of shoes that didn't fit me right and hurt my feet. If I complained about them, he would just say that they needed to be worn more to stretch them out. I couldn't wear tank tops or clothing that showed my skin because he was worried about getting skin cancer. I had to wear a hat all the time for the same reason.

There were certain retail stores that I was not allowed to shop in because of his political beliefs. He would know if I went to these forbidden places because he would track my every move from my cell phone. I was told it was for my safety, but it was really to see where I was. Not that I was doing anything weird. I didn't even attempt it because he would lecture me for hours if he caught me doing something that he didn't approve.

My money was tightly controlled. I had such bad anxiety about going grocery shopping that it made me physically sick to my stomach. There was only a small amount of money given to me to buy food and household supplies, but I was expected to make gourmet meals. When I had to drive long distances for work, I was not permitted to buy a drink or snacks at a gas station. I was told that it was too expensive and had to pack my own drinks and snacks.

Our cars were old and consistently needed maintenance. A new car was not permitted because supposedly it would cost too much. We had the money. He just wanted to spend it on other things that he felt were more important. Here I was, a high-end makeup artist, charging a ton of money, and sometimes working with very wealthy people, driving an ugly, junky old truck. I was so embarrassed that I would park down the street or in a different area if I thought anyone was going to see it. I hated going anywhere because of my vehicle.

My diet was heavily controlled too. While yes, it is important to eat healthily, I have a lot of digestive issues and many foods bother my stomach. That didn't matter to him, and he wanted me to eat the foods that he liked. My severe stomach pain did not matter. I am petite, healthy, and slim, but he and his mother would lecture me regularly about my diet. I never understood what I was doing that was so wrong.

I began to discover there was a deep sadness in me that I had been suppressing. It never occurred to me to end the relationship, mostly because I was absolutely terrified of the divorce process and couldn't even fathom going through it. I was 40, had no savings, was deep in debt because of his poor financial decisions, and had nowhere to go. I figured that I had made my bed, now I had to lie in it and suffer for the rest of my life.

I dealt with the unhappiness by punishing myself in various ways. I exercised every day for long periods until I was completely exhausted. The music I listened to was dark, full of anger and hate. My escape was to play fantasy games on my computer and zone out of my world. I drank more alcohol in the evening when he permitted me to drink, sometimes sneaking an extra whiskey shot without him knowing. I didn't care about anything. I just wanted to withdraw from my sad life.

Something snapped inside me one day. A friend of mine had observed some verbal abuse towards me, which was usually well hidden from everybody. My friend said to me in a sincere and caring way, "You shouldn't be treated this way." It sunk in that he was absolutely right. What was I doing? I didn't deserve this treatment and wasn't going to take it anymore. Although I had no plan for what I was going to do about every aspect of my life, I realized that I had to tell him that I wanted a divorce. It was the most frightening thing that I would ever face.

My stomach felt like it was in my knees and my whole body was shaking, but one morning, out came the words, "I want a divorce." Those were the hardest words that I have ever said in my life, but I did it. The wrath came down on me immediately once my words sunk into him. He was furious. I threw some clothes in a small packing crate and left within five minutes, so I didn't have to suffer the onslaught of verbal abuse.

After staying in a hotel for a few days, he convinced me to come home to "talk" with him. There was no talking on my part, and it was just him lecturing me for hours about what a terrible person I was and how I was ruining his life. He told me that I would be a divorcee in her 40's and nobody would ever love me again. What a terrible thing to say. At that point, I knew I had to go forward, no matter what.

The fear of the unknown terrified me. Where was I going to live? What was I going to do? How was I going to completely start over at 40 years old? I left with very few things – just my personal belongings, a few beloved kitchen items, and my sports equipment. I took the crappy little truck too.

Every day I tackled one small hurdle at a time. The first thing that I did was go out and get a new car, which was beyond exciting. I even got to drive it out of the showroom floor at the car dealership. I loved it and cruised around with the sunroof open, letting the sunshine hit my bare shoulders because I could finally wear a tank top again. Luckily, at that time I had plenty of weddings booked, so I had a steady source of income – money for which I worked my tail off. And it was all mine now.

What took me a while to realize was that I had been thoroughly brainwashed. My habits were not healthy and I needed to re-train my brain. It was now okay to go to buy whatever I liked at the grocery store, even if it cost a little more. I could go to the gas station and buy a drink and some snacks when traveling. I could wear new clothes and shoes, the kind that I loved. Even though I still had nightmares from the mental abuse I'd endured for so long, I was finally starting to become happy. It felt like the world's weight had lifted off my body and my wings finally were allowed to spread out. I felt like shouting to the world, "I'M FREE!"

A lot of stigma goes along with getting a divorce. Many people view divorced people as failures. I was nervous and ashamed to tell people, especially those who thought my husband was the greatest man in the world. Most people had no idea how poorly I was treated for so many years. The first person that I told about my divorce was my mother. I was in my new car, driving to work and had her on my fancy new car speakerphone. She didn't respond for about 30 seconds, then said, "Oh Tracy, thank God!" I cried in relief.

My relationships with my family and long-lost friends began to mend, which made me incredibly happy. But not all reactions were positive. What really saddened me was the backlash that I received from colleagues and friends that I shared with my ex-husband. They unfriended me on Facebook and all social media. I was painted as a bad person; they wouldn't talk to me or even look at when I had to work with some of them. They completely shunned me, and that made me feel terrible. None of these people knew what our personal relationship was like behind closed doors. I didn't understand. How could people judge you for doing something to better your life? I had to change my thinking before it drove me crazy. If they didn't want to be my friend now, then they had never really been my friend to begin with, and I didn't need them. It was difficult, but I now know that getting over the debilitating fear and getting a divorce was one of the best things that I ever did.

My life now is happy and free. My thinking has changed tremendously in the past two years, and I know I can overcome any fear or life obstacle that comes my way. My jewelry business is thriving and I love working from home now. Looking back, I realize that, in a way, going on "lockdown" was an incredibly important pivot point in my working and personal life. Spending time with my family and our precious golden retriever made me understand how meaningful relationships are. They mean much more than money or social status.

Working from home has been a bit of an adjustment, but I have come up with a routine to keep me from getting distracted. I get up early in the morning, have breakfast and maybe watch the news, mostly for the weather report. Then I get to work tidying up the house and myself before I go to work. When I arrive in my office, the first task is getting all my jewelry orders from the previous day packaged up and shipped out so that my customers get them as fast as possible. The rest of my day is spent selling live, creating listings for the items that I have to sell, doing inventory, ordering new products and organizing my jewelry room. I also interact directly with my customers every day, making sure everybody is satisfied with my services.

The rest of my day is up to my family and me. If we feel like going out for a hike, we do it. If we need to take

Sunday off to relax and spend extra time together, we do that. Working from home and being my own boss has been a beautiful transition for me, and I have never felt freer and happier.

In starting over with my new business, Eric and I also came up with the idea that we should move out of our area and try something new. We felt it was time to go somewhere else, live a peaceful life, sell our jewelry, and enjoy ourselves. Since I work from home now, our house can be anywhere. The area where we live now has a lot of what I call "bad juju," and is filled with memories of rough times. It's time to release ourselves from the burden of all the negativity and build new positive memories.

We currently live in the mountains of Utah, USA, at 10,000-foot elevation. The snowfall here is incredible, with a long season of bitterly cold days. In deciding where to go, my only demand was that it was somewhere warm where we wouldn't have to shovel snow for six months of the year. Out of the blue, Eric said, "Let's go to the beach in Texas." I agreed immediately. I only thought about it for maybe one second. My new attitude is not to be afraid, but just to say, "Why not?"

We found a house that we liked online and went to look at immediately. It was love at first sight. Neither of us had ever even been to the beach in Texas before, but the adventure of it sounded exciting. We purchased the home after only visiting the area for less than 24 hours.

The fear of the unknown is always there, but that won't stop us from moving. Yes, there are hurricanes in that area, there is flooding. There are snakes and all sorts of large creepy insects that we aren't used to. The climate is humid and hot, the opposite of where we live now. My hair is going to be a mess. We will be going from an elevation of 10,000 feet to an altitude of 10 feet. Everything will be different, except for us and our positive attitude. We will plan well and adapt to our new situation. Other people can do it, so why not us? Living in fear of hurricanes or creepy critters is no way to thrive, there are bad things on every part of the planet, you just learn to live with them.

Of course, while most of our friends and family have been positive about our announced move to Texas, there are always those with negative comments, no matter what we do. I choose to ignore the haters. Their opinion really doesn't matter. It's our life, not theirs. We must do what's best for us and that's what makes for a happy, healthy, fun experience.

Many years ago, I saw a story on our local news station where they were doing a short segment for the anniversary of D-Day. They were interviewing an older man who was in the Army and fought in World War II. The reporter asked him what the secret to life was. He responded, "The secret to life is to be happy." I don't know why this man's simple statement made such an impact on me. He had evidently seen so many terrible things and he was still happy. I vowed to live my life and be happy like him.

To this day, I still say that getting divorced was the best thing that I ever did. I couldn't imagine what I would be like if I never got the nerve to stand up for myself. It was a horrible process, but I survived and am thriving now, because I overcame my fears.

My favorite part of my new business now is the impact that I have made on other people's lives. My jewelry makes my customers feel pretty and my heart bursts with joy when they send me little love messages saying how important we made them feel. Having a mentor also really helped me get out of my own head and try different strategies. She continually helps me reach new goals and strive to be better.

With my makeup business, looking at an empty calendar was the most frightening thing in the world. Now I am relieved to see a blank calendar. It means that I have time to work at home with be my family. I overcame the fear of losing my whole makeup business and turning it into a positive, life-changing event.

If the secret to life really is as simple as being happy, then conquering fearful obstacles in life is necessary to reach that incredible level of happiness. I now hope to inspire others to empower themselves to seek freedom, love and joy in life. The journey may be rough, but the outcome is pure bliss.

"Fight your fears and you'll be in a battle forever. Face your fears and you'll be free forever."

~ Lucas Jonkman

CHAPTER FOUR

—◆—

The Peril Of Fear In
The Creation Of Reality

By Jan De Smet

T he cell door closed behind him, and he said, "I am going to beat the shit out of you." He was a 195 cm tall Aboriginal who weighed over 160 kg, was about 25 years old, and full of rage. He expected me to get scared and try to run or fight. Spontaneously, I asked him to explain to me why I deserved to be beaten up? He told me it was to teach me a lesson, so I would not kick the wall anymore and disturb his sleep. I explained that I was probably hitting the wall with my knees when I turned over in my bed. I suggested that he ask the prison guards for an extra mattress or pillow to put against the wall which could stop the noise that woke him up. The staunch, raging Aboriginal mumbled something and walked out of the jail cell. I noticed that I had felt no fear in this scary situation, and that's exactly why this went so well. Fear attracts what we fear, I thought.

Later that day, he saw me in the yard and asked me to walk with him. I felt safer as the yard is not the place where they "teach you a lesson." Tears welled in his eyes as he thanked me for dealing with him the way I had. He explained that when sentenced for six months, he had received an additional two years for assaults on other prisoners and was fearful of never getting out. He became protective of me. I had touched his humanity in a world that is not sympathetic towards gentle emotions. The social structure in jail is entwined with fear that can make or break one who lacks fortitude. If I had gotten scared and reacted as a fearful person, I would have been physically bashed. Jail beatings are not merciful. The beatings don't stop when the person is on the ground because of fear — fear that he is going to get back up and beat you, fear he will tell the jailers... Fear is actually the cause of the event you're afraid of, so by not getting fearful, I avoided the normal cycle of events.

In a world like the maximum-security prison, fear is the primary emotion that controls daily life — your social position, to a large extent. I had learned that when I ended up in jail a few months earlier. I was 43 when I went to prison for the first time. Going to jail was something I had always been terrified of. I was so scared that I went on the run for over a year. The funny thing is that I studied criminology and never expected to end up on this side of the prison gates. I was also educated enough to know that going on the run was not solving anything but only making it worse. Internally, my fear proved stronger than my rational mind.

The Courier Mail headlines stated, "Arrest warrant out for 'Porn king" and "Porn King skips bail', police are looking for him…" It's very stressful being on the run. You are rubber necking, always scanning for the authorities. In the end, the system catches up with you. Part of me was relieved that it was over, but the fear was not over yet. You have a fear of being in jail but also about your looming sentence. I was looking at a sentence of between six months and six years jail time. I was at the University of Anxiety, and I decided to do my best to graduate. The fear of a conviction was big but not unbearable; after all, I was guilty of the charges of possession of drugs and guns. Years later, I was in jail, charged with crimes I did not commit, and I found it was harder to deal with! When you go to prison, awaiting trial for crimes you did not commit, that's hard. You are so angry and fearful at the same time, and everything is confusing. Most people in jail claim they are innocent, and you start to fear a wrongful conviction after hearing their stories day after day. Almost every felon justifies his actions and feels innocent; at times it's laughable to what extent they create a rationale that makes them almost a victim.

I became so nervous and scared that the fear became unbearable, and when it became too much to handle, I received the answer. Nothing is more unpleasant than being afraid. I was afraid of fear itself! I found my way out of fear by accepting that I had an accident with the law and might have to spend eight years in jail for a crime I did not commit. If you have an accident on the road and end up in a wheelchair, that is unfair, but it is reality. I had been on a collision with the law and thought, it's better being in jail than in a wheelchair. So, by accepting the position I was in, I found peace. I saw how people who had a traffic accident and end up paraplegic have more to complain about than me, who had a collision with the law. The fear fell off me, and a peaceful feeling took its place. They say that fear stands for 'Future Expectations Appearing Real'. By the surrender to the mishap and the acceptance of the consequences, I had let go of the future expectation of getting justice with a not guilty verdict.

The World Of Fear

When you have never been to jail, all you know is what you have seen on TV, where the strong prey on the weak, and fear is their tool. It's a daunting experience! As soon as you walk into that cell or yard, it's there. As soon as that gate closes behind you, inmates come up to you to size you up. It's very primitive behavior at its rawest. It pays to be the first out of the starting blocks and measure up the new inmate; if he takes the bait and shows fear, it will cost him. They will ask for a smoke, and if they feel he is intimidated into giving a smoke, they'll get the whole pack off him. If he hands over his whole pack, they will see if he has anything else of value like shoes, etc. When he has given away all his valuables, they will ask him what medication he is receiving because certain drugs are valuable to them. They will make him hand them over by using intimidation — and the last thing of value is your arse, literally. So, getting scared is not the solution, nor is giving away your things and medication to bring you peace. You can't fake it. This is the University of Fear. These people can smell fear and will know if you pretend that you're fearless. Fear is the currency. Fear is the system. Fear is what makes the difference between doing time and doing hard time. The fearful are getting stood over, having a very difficult experience in there. For the fearless, it's a journey that comes a lot easier. It's a difficult dilemma to find yourself in; you are terrified of jail, and if you cannot lose the fear right away, you will have a hell of a time. But necessity creates ability, and when the pressure was at its most significant, I reacted like I never anticipated I would. In this situation there was no time to think, and what you do and say just flows.

It was my first week in jail, and so far, things went well until one particular morning. An inmate I did not know walked into our two-person cell. He told my cellmate Victor to ' Fuck off'!. Victor looked at me and asked me what I wanted him to do. I said, "Close the door behind you and stand in front of it." That slightly unsettled the intruder. I said, "Shall we talk first or fight first? Maybe talking first is the smartest. We can still fight if we can't sort it out; what's the hurry? What is it you want?" He wanted the oxycontin opiate painkillers I was given daily for my back. He explained he was a heroin addict and needed the opiates more than I did. I told him, "Giving them to you is not a long-term solution because tomorrow, if someone bigger and stronger than you wants them, the issue continues. If it creates envy, I will go without the medication if it's going to give me problems here, but I won't give them to anyone." I contacted the nurse and said I didn't need the medication anymore. The whole druggie gang didn't get it. They would do anything to get that medication, and I was getting it but was willing to walk away from it. As confused as they were, I did earn their respect… or had I just unsettled them? They started calling me the dark horse — the one you can't predict — and left me in peace. I had decided not to play along in their games. This is not the way things normally work. Mostly, it is the start of a battle of the fearful. He who gets scared first, loses! And if he can't scare or beat you alone, he will come back with another junkie and go again. In this world of endless boredom, it's one way to spend your days. In there, being physically strong is only getting you that far or that safe; it's more the willingness to go all the way that makes you an unattractive target.

Born Full Of Fear

Fear is common and runs deep in my family. I was a soldier, as was my father, grandfathers, and great grandfathers. My dad's father was in the German concentration camps. My mum's father had his farm taken by the SS, the paramilitary organization under direct control of Adolph Hitler, who made it their headquarters. My family suffered the effects of hunger and war for many generations. It creates trans-generational post-traumatic stress disorder (PTSD). As a result, I was a terrified little boy who battled fear all his life. I did all the things that scared me so that I could lose the fear. I was afraid of violence, so I did full-contact kickboxing. I was scared of heights, so I went mountain climbing and flew small planes. I conquered my fears, one by one, and learned that there is nothing to be scared of other than fear itself. Feeling fear is such an unpleasant emotion. It's uncomfortable because it's terrible for your health, thus we receive it as a signal from our body. Worry causes stress, high blood pressure, strokes, depression, and more. Each of us has a defense mechanism to deal with fear. I do what scares me until it doesn't scare me anymore, which has led me to have quite an adventurous life. I was diagnosed with severe PTSD when I was 46 years old. Part is trans-generational stress which set me up with a predisposition, and part is from chewing off more than I could swallow.

Chewing Off Too Much

In 1999, I migrated from Belgium to Australia with my wife and two young children of one and a half and three years old. I migrated partly out of fear and a few different concerns. I had made over ten million dollars but never paid any tax. It was a fun game to outsmart the tax system, but the fear was catching up with me. Because I had so much success, I was scared of failing. I was frightened for the safety of my offspring! Belgium has a high population density and has historically been in so many wars and conflicts that I did not see it as a safe place for my children in the long term. After we moved to Australia, my marriage didn't last long. In 2003, my wife left me and took the children with her. She played legal court games for years, which resulted in me not seeing my children for an extended period of time. It was an emotionally hard, being alone on the other side of the world; I had no family at all in Australia, no friends, and no support systems. It was a time where I cried every morning. Missing my young children was extremely painful.

I began to self-medicate with all sorts of drugs. Speed, ice, cocaine, and ecstasy were my preferred ones. I had started adult entertainment centers, adult shops, peepshows, adult cinema, and swinging venues. The money was excellent, and I lived a life of sex, drugs, and rock and roll, as they call it. I was perceived to be a gangster. You see such things on TV, but they don't often show the flip side — it was a very lonely life. You have lots of sex, enhanced by drugs, but you develop no emotional connections. You have lots of people who want to be your friend, but you know deep inside why they want you as their friend. In a sex-starved society where so many men are desperately seeking intense and freeing sexuality, I was the epitome of hedonistic promiscuity. Most evenings I would end up in the old nightclub above the swinger's club/peepshow, and drug-enhanced sex was the best thing to keep the boredom with life and the pain of loneliness at bay. I had become a party animal in party central, the king of the party in the nightlife district. Inside I was not happy, but I kept myself from falling into a deep hole. Of course, such a life is the envy of many that don't know any better.

I don't envy anyone in such a life; I feel pity for them, if anything. It was mainly the gangsters and bike gangs who felt these types of businesses should belong to them. They tried to scare me into selling it to them for peanuts. They tried extortion, stand over, protection fees, and anything else they have in their cruel, primitive power-sick approach to life. I was no gangster or criminal, and I had no connections to such a milieu. I was not someone you could scare away. There is nothing I hate more than being scared, so I reacted like a bull charging a red flag and would go into a counterattack. That battle went on for a few years, and I have hundreds of stories from that era. One of these events is relevant to the culmination of peak fear and how I dealt with it.

Under Attack: A Rabbit And The Fox

To understand this event, I have to explain how living with PTSD for most of your life and how transgenerational stress disorder causes you to develop certain coping mechanisms. One of those coping mechanisms that often develops in children living with levels of overwhelming fear is the ability to "scan" others for their emotional state and thoughts. I feel it when someone has negative feelings towards me if that person is in relative proximity. I feel it when someone is about to throw a punch! And this gift had often saved my skin because I could avoid the situation before it developed into something unpleasant. The biker gangs had found the weakest link. I had a partner, a minority shareholder (5%), and under pressure, he sided with a bike gang. He had tried to lock me out of my own business and had planned to keep me locked out with the help of a hard-core bikie security man on site. With the company making over $15K net profit per week, they could play court games for years and keep me at bay while they milked the cow, or that was the plan at least. I hired another gang of big tough Maori guys and paid them to help me take the business back physically, and I would ask the court to issue an injunction order in the days after I took back possession of my business. We took possession of the company and changed the locks. Due to the amount of muscle I had brought along, the take-back went smoothly. The cops arrived and most of the Maori muscle ended up getting arrested, most on outstanding warrants. But I ended up in possession of my business and office.

It was tense, but it was fun, and winning is always uplifting. I informed my legal team what had happened, and a hearing was planned to get the injunction order. I was living in Red Hill, and my house had been targeted in a drive-by shooting to intimidate me into selling the businesses at a ridiculous price. To deal with the stress and fear, I was increasingly using more and more amphetamines. I was also always well armed.

This particular morning, the matter was set to appear before a judge, I was awake very early. Like a proper addict, I had some amphetamines for breakfast. Around 6 am, I saw the outlines of a huge man through the side window. He was taller than the peach tree in the garden. I wasn't thinking properly. The speed makes you too confident. I could have taken a closer look; I could have had my pistol or sawed off shotgun at the ready. But I did not. Cocky as I was, I opened the door.

I saw several big burly men, and I understood right away what they were coming for. They were coming to beat me up so badly that I would end up in the hospital that day, not in the court room. If I had displayed fear, things would have gone terribly wrong and painful for me. There was no time to think. So, I heard myself say, "Come on in, I'll put the kettle on. It's better to talk business then taking shit to the courts." I swung the front door open, stepped aside to let them in, and put the kettle on. I said,

"I'm just going to collect the mail and the milk." Since I was totally calm and displayed no fear or stress, the trick worked. I was in my underwear, t-shirt, and barefoot.

The mailbox was 15 meters from the front door, so I just kept walking past the milk and mail. walking towards Musgrave Rd. Halfway towards the main road, there where another two thugs waiting, and by that time, the steroid monsters in my house had woken up to the fact I had tricked them. They yelled out to the other two men who were making their way towards my home. I was able to knock the first one out very fast. The second one was a hard fighter and I was knocked down, but on amphetamines, one does not feel much pain or tiredness, nor do you get knocked out easily; people on amphetamines are every bouncer's worst nightmare. I got back up, kicked him in the chest, and he fell back, giving me enough time to run to the main road. I was bleeding and had lost my t-shirt in the fight. I stood in the middle of the road with my arms spread wide, jumping in front of the first car. The soldier from Enoggera who was driving the car was cool and drove me to Brisbane City Police Station. The police treated me with suspicion — "The boy who cried wolf," they said. I asked them to escort me home so I could get my clothes and documents. They escorted me to the court and happened to notice that the ex-business partner who was the subject of the injunction order had not even bothered to seek legal representation, thinking I would not turn up for court.

When I got back home later that day, it hit me. I was shit scared. I discovered I felt like a vulnerable little rabbit, hunted and scared. I felt that such events could do lasting damage to my mental health. It did get worse. Even with a gun in each hand, I felt scared and could hardly sleep. By the morning, I realized that living in fear is hell and I would not be able to live like that. As was my usual way to deal with fear, I went head-on and did terrifying things. I contacted the ex-business partner who lost the injunction and asked to talk business. He was reluctant and scared but agreed to meet in the Queen Street Mall, in public, where he would be safe. We sat down, and I put my Glock 9mm under a newspaper and shoved that towards him. I explained the gun was loaded and that I was prepared to die. I proposed to walk in front of him wherever he guided me and told him that I was happy to die but could not accept cowards who send others to do their dirty work. I was prepared to die but not to live in constant fear. He did not have the balls to shoot me, as I expected. I explained to him that this was his very last chance and, if he did not take the opportunity, there would be consequences. If I ever saw or even expected him or his cronies anywhere in my life, I would kill him. I explained that I can't accept to live in fear but can accept to die. My fearlessness freaked him out as he saw my determination and brave decision not to live in fear. I don't believe that a life full of fear is worth living. It's too scary! Death, on the other hand is peaceful, or so I believe.

I bought a ute and installed a 1000-liter drum and pump on the back, filled it with a mixture of petrol and diesel, and went to the bikies' clubhouse on a club night. I took along a very scary-looking dude and paid him to do nothing, say nothing, and just stand three meters behind me to cover my back. I gave him an earpiece to make it look more organized than it was. I tucked my two handguns under my belt, making sure they were visible. I went to the bar and told the barman that I needed to speak to the club president and sergeant of arms. He said they were not available. I asked him to take a look at the ute I parked outside the clubhouse and told him that if I leave without talking to the people in charge, I would pump the 700-liter fuel on their clubhouse, and I put my sawed-off shotgun on the bar. It didn't take long before the leaders came forward. I told them of the events last week and explained that I can't live in fear and that I choose to get it over and done with. Every man has a breaking point, and I had reached mine. I explained that there were two choices possible: one is battling it out here and now or we could make an agreement. I proposed they speak to their members to let them know they all had to leave me alone in every possible way, now and forever. I also explained the consequences of not adhering to the agreement, and I had planned on keeping the fire truck for a while. They agreed and said they respected a man that stood up as I did.

When I look back, I realize that making someone scared is very dangerous — nobody likes to be scared. There are very few ways to deal with fear, and most are on the internal level. There are only two basic emotions: love and fear. As humans, we are destined to find our love and become the love that we are and always have been. When fear rules, love wilts. A life with love is a life well-lived; a life in fear is not a life worth living. Many people in history have sacrificed their lives to get rid of dictators that rule with fear. It's a common human characteristic to refuse to live in fear and be willing to die for the freedom of having to live in fear of others. I sold the business shortly after all the gangsters had given up and moved on to a more peaceful environment and activities. I am happy I experienced the world of gangsters and motorcycle gangs. I am happy I experienced the world of incarceration. But I am way happier to now live the simple life of a farmer.

I don't know if it was because I was a slow learner or because my fears were so deeply ingrained in my psyche that I had to experience so many extreme situations. What I do know is that nothing scares me anymore except fear itself. Love is the answer. When I look back to the most intense moments of my life — that fraction of a second where you don't have time to think about your response or actions — they all seem to have one thing in common: I felt a divine spirit was guiding me through all of them, and it was not my brain or thinking that came up with the words I spoke at those moments. I believe a guardian angel or divine force was on my side to allow me to experience those events and learn the lessons I needed to. Despite the intense life I lived, I feel as clean as a virgin and untouched as a newborn.

The world has not tainted my soul. When I left that city life behind, I was still edgy and alert with all the symptoms of PTSD. My psychiatrist advised me to go live somewhere remote and do something with animals. I met a beautiful woman — a mother of three children — and we went to live on a large farm, a half hour drive to the nearest neighbors. I bought two pups from a very protective bloodline and trained them as guard dogs and personal protectors, Luna and Tic. They gave me lots of peace and good sleep. Breeding and training assistance and protection dogs became our hobby and business. The satisfaction of providing people with a four-legged friend is much greater than providing people with adult entertainment.

My way of dealing with fear was not different than that of most people. We accept and live with it. Somewhere in puberty, that changed. I took fear head on and did the things that scared me. I created, participated in many scary events and situations. I overcame my fears by going into them, by experiencing them, and they fell away. God does not throw anything at us that we cannot handle. We learn mental tricks and park our emotions in closed compartments. It was a dangerous and intense journey and I would not dare to advise such a path, but I did come out the other end with very little fear. The absence of fear makes space for love, and I am living with a lot of love in my being with a lot of beings with a lot of love around me. Knowing where it brought me, I would walk that path again. There is nothing to fear but fear itself! Fear is all about the expectations of the future, and the more we learn to live in the now, there is no fear in the now. Some situations were so intense that they forced me in the now, as the time to anticipate the future was not available. That confirms the fact that there is nothing to fear.

**"Face your fears and they will
lose their power over you."**

~ Gill Washington

CHAPTER FIVE

❖

On The Other Side Of Fear

By Susan Dampier

Writing this chapter has been quite an emotional experience for me. Looking back at moments that I had long ago tucked away brought back vivid feelings of sadness and uncertainty. There have been so many times throughout my life when I doubted my strength and ability to persevere, and yet, here I am today. I believe we all have moments such as these when we don't quite know how we will make it through, and yet we do. There's a good chance your greatest moments of struggle once loomed before you like giant, insurmountable hills, and yet when you look back today, those giant hills probably look like tiny pebbles along the road from who you once were to who you are today. Am I right?

Life has a funny way of doing that — allowing us to forget the things that matter, and yet we can remember some things that seem so insignificant with great detail. I can remember so vividly the excitement I would feel on summer mornings as a child. I grew up in New Jersey, and we always slept with the windows open. The tract houses in the neighborhood where my grandparents' house stood were built in the early 1950s, and the central air conditioner wasn't a common luxury back then. I would lie still in the bed, between the cool white sheets, and listen to the birds sing in the Dogwood tree just outside my bedroom window. My eyes would open slowly, and I'd watch small particles of dust dance in the golden sunlight filtered between the branches and into the room. As a small child, no detail escaped me. I think that's how it is for most children; everything is new, and what may go unnoticed by an adult is spectacular and interesting to a child.

As an adult, my mornings took on an entirely different set of emotions. The excitement I had felt long ago was replaced by exhaustion and fantasies of crawling back into bed later that night. I would often wonder if this was normal. Does everyone feel like this, or is it just me? From the outside looking in, I had a lot to be happy about. In my early forties, I was a wife to a great man, a mother to four wonderful kids. I had a successful 20-year career in finance, a beautiful house…on paper, I was living "The American Dream." But what exactly is The American Dream?

It's something I have often pondered, and it seems to me that most people (and I was one of them) forget all about the dreams they once had. The hopes and the inspirations that once caused butterflies to dance in their bellies are ever so slowly replaced by an existence that no longer inspires. Why does this happen?

I had simply given up on the belief that the dreams I once had for myself would ever come true. Of course, some of them did — I had a beautiful family, a house, a job — but I'm talking about those inspiring dreams I had long ago.

As a young child, I was raised by my grandparents. My grandfather doted on me and spoiled me, as many grandparents do. My mother lived across our tiny town on the Jersey shore with my younger brother, 11 months my junior. My father was a merchant mariner and worked out of a port in Florida, so he spent most of his time down there. Whenever I questioned why I didn't live with my parents as other kids did, my grandparents would tell me that my parents dropped me off after I came home from the hospital, and I just ended up staying with them. If I asked my mother, she would say that my grandparents kept me and wouldn't give me back. It's a strange thing that all my life, I never really thought much about the effects of being told from a young age that I was unwanted by my parents.

At the age of ten, my mother decided that she would relocate to Florida with my brother to be with my father. I think there must have been some talk amongst the adults about me moving with them. I know I asked to go, but the decision was made for me to remain in New Jersey with my grandparents. I remember the day my family left. It was summertime and the school year had just ended. I knew my parents were leaving, and I was so sad. I wanted to go; I didn't want them to leave me behind, but I could do or say nothing to change the inevitable. They were driving my mom's big yellow Oldsmobile down to Florida and would be leaving that night.

As the afternoon winded down, I begged them to please take me. They promised I would come down soon, maybe later that summer, once they got settled. Even though I didn't live with my mother and brother, I still saw them both every day. I was used to my father not being around. It was that way my whole life. But knowing my mother and brother would be gone was very difficult. As the car pulled away down the street, I remember chasing after it, running out of my little wooden Dr. Scholl's sandals, crying and begging them to stop. But they didn't. And when I couldn't run anymore, I just stood in the street, barefoot and broken-hearted, and watched as their taillights got further and further away.

I never did visit them that summer, and before I knew it, school was back in session. I missed seeing my parents and brother and often rode my bike to a payphone at the grocery store around the corner to call them and beg them to let me live with them. I didn't want to hurt my grandparents' feelings, but I wanted to be with my parents and felt that they wouldn't understand.

The following summer, I was allowed to go to Florida for a visit, with the intention that I would return at the end of the summer. Instead, I decided to stay in Florida and not return to New Jersey. This was the beginning of a period of significant dysfunction in my life.

My parents had a tumultuous relationship, and my father spent a great deal of time away from home, out to sea. Neither of my parents was responsible with money; they enjoyed gambling and alcohol, which meant that more often than not, there was too much month and not enough money. These are things that, to some point, I was aware of. I knew my parents drank and partied a lot. Gambling was a favorite pastime for most of my family; however, because I lived with my grandparents, I hadn't been previously subjected to the day-to-day effects of living like this. It was not uncommon for us to have the water, phone, or electricity turned off. I can recall running away to my friend's house because I didn't want to be home without lights and running water. Throughout my entire childhood, it was a common occurrence that my parents would take their jewelry or other valuables to various pawnshops to pay bills. Being exposed to these types of behaviors created the foundation of a scarcity mindset that I would carry with me into adulthood.

I can remember one Thanksgiving when I was in my thirties where a family member looked inside my pantry and commented at the amount of food it contained. Up to that point, I had never considered that my pantry and freezer were always overflowing with food, as was the second refrigerator in my garage. As a teenager, one of my girlfriends had a pantry like this — stocked with every snack and chip and cookie you can imagine. The first time I saw it, I was in awe and thought, "They are so rich!" At that moment, I made a mental note that I wanted to have a bountiful pantry like that one day. Fast forward twenty years, I turned around and stood before the full shelves in my kitchen and felt a sense of peace looking at them. Having food made me feel secure.

As a teen, I always dreamed of growing up to be successful. I can remember saving every Cosmopolitan magazine issue in high school and imagining living in a big city, taking amazing vacations, and having an exciting career. However, my reality was far from that fantasy. I lived in a small Florida community that didn't have much industry outside of tourism. In my circle of influence growing up, if you wanted to earn more than minimum wage, you became a waitress, a topless dancer, or a drug dealer.

At around the age of 14, I realized that if I wanted to have more in my future, I needed to take responsibility for my actions and life. The first three years of living with my mother and father in Florida was a difficult transition. I developed a strong sense of resentment toward them for the lack of stability we had, but there was nothing I could do, so I checked out. I stopped doing schoolwork, going from a straight-A student to straight-F. I started smoking and skipping school, often getting into fights with other kids. This went on for several years as the situation at home continued to spiral out of control.

The year prior, our family moved into a gorgeous two-story home on a lagoon a few blocks away from the beach. Both my brother and I were so excited to be living in a big, newer home. The excitement didn't last very long, as my father was away much of the time we lived there, and my mother struggled to keep the house afloat. We lived there for about a year, and I can recall telling visitors that we were waiting for our furniture to be delivered because our living room was bare, without even a chair. My parents were going through some serious challenges at this time that I was unaware of. All I knew is that we didn't have any furniture, we never had any money, and we didn't have utilities from time to time.

One day, without warning or notice, my parents told us that we were going to be moving. This time, instead of staying on the little barrier island beach community where we lived, we moved across the bridge to the main island. I didn't want to go, and leave behind the friends and familiarity I had grown accustomed to, but I had no choice. A few weeks later, there was a knock at the door, and the people who owned the house we were renting had come to take it back over. The house was owned by a young couple who had moved away, and their parents managed the property. That day, the four of them showed up as a unified team to make sure we vacated the premises. We were being evicted.

We weren't really prepared to go, only a box here and there had been packed. All of a sudden, there was a flurry of activity. The mother of the young woman made her way in and started bringing things outside to the front lawn. I remember standing by the front door just watching this blonde-haired stranger breeze by me like I didn't exist. Maybe she didn't see me because I wanted nothing more than to fade into the background. As she made her way back outside with a belonging that I can't remember today, I looked up to see the young woman who owned the home looking at me. She was so pretty, I thought, with her straight blond hair pulled back into a neat ponytail. I don't recall her exact features, but I'll never forget how she looked at me. She felt sorry for me. She was embarrassed to be there, to be the one to eject a family with young children from her home.

That move was a turning point in my life. I saw it as an opportunity for a fresh start. Although we only moved five miles inland, it may as well have been five hundred miles for a thirteen-year-old. A different school, a different town...Without much in the way of parental guidance and encouragement, I committed to excel in school. I became extremely focused and obsessive about doing well. Looking back, I believe it was because the rest of my life was in chaos, and this was something that I could control. During this period, the relationship I had with my parents was stable for the most part, but still extremely dysfunctional. My dad was out to sea most of the time, and my mother did the best she could but was not equipped for the job of parenting two teens on her own. My younger brother was like a stranger to me in many ways. As we entered high school, we didn't socialize with the same groups of people, and although we lived in the same house, we didn't have much of a relationship.

As a teen, I had no way of knowing or understanding how this environment shaped patterns for relationships and behavior that I would carry with me into adulthood. Looking back, I can recognize that my longing for stability, security, and love, often led me to make impetuous decisions based on feeling rather than common sense. I was afraid to be alone, afraid to fail, afraid to be poor, afraid to be judged, afraid to be wrong...this list goes on and on.

I had my first child, a daughter, shortly after high school and found myself a single mother at the age of 20. I didn't want to stay in Florida, so I decided to move back to New Jersey and returned to live with my grandparents. My uncle worked at a bank, and I was able to secure a bank teller position. I was so grateful to have a job that paid more than minimum wage and provided benefits. The bank I worked at was located across the street from a large brokerage firm. I was always friendly with the financial advisors who banked with us, and I was encouraged to apply for a job there, which I did. I was 21, and transitioning from a bank teller to a brokerage sales assistant was the beginning of my career in the financial services industry. I was fortunate that a college diploma wasn't required at the time, and getting my foot in the door allowed me to work my way up the corporate ladder. Over the next 22 years, I worked in various positions with various firms and created a successful career; however, behind the facade of success lingered some of the same dysfunctions of my formative years.

I got married at the age of 24 to a young man who came from an affluent family. Though our families and upbringing couldn't be any more different, we were both similar in that we had a lot of unresolved hurt and damage from childhood that we carried with us into our marriage. He was everything I thought I ever wanted in a husband: loving, handsome, from a great family. He adopted my daughter when she was five, and we went on to have three more children together. For the first eight years of our marriage, we had more than our fair share of ups and downs but we always made it through. I was wholeheartedly committed to our marriage, and despite periods of great turmoil, we stayed together for nearly 14 years.

It was so hard to let go of that relationship. We were both very codependent, and underneath all the pain, there was always the hope that things could get better. The divorce was one of the most traumatic experiences of my life, and there were moments throughout the process when I had never felt more lonely or afraid. I suffered from debilitating anxiety and second-guessed my decision to move forward with my life so often. Ultimately, we both knew we couldn't stay together; too much damage had been done. After extensive therapy and counseling, we decided to end the marriage.

A divorce is like a death in many ways — the loss of all the hopes and dreams, the ideas of what could have been and should have been but weren't; that was something I struggled with for a long time. I never thought I'd get divorced; however, I saw firsthand from my parents what happens when people stay together for all the wrong reasons. My mother and father were an example of this. There was no trust or respect within their relationship. Although they remained married, it created a great deal of animosity and resentment amongst them towards one another.

My mother would later tell me that my father dealt with a great deal of inner-turmoil and anger in the last years of his life. He was unhappy and would often say that he hated his life. He died unexpectedly in 2010 following a heart attack and subsequent stroke. I believe that the weight of his life and all his choices and regrets is what finally broke his heart.

I didn't want this for my life. I didn't wish to have days filled with turmoil, dysfunction, and animosity. I didn't want to stay in a marriage "for the kids" because I experienced firsthand the damage that such an arrangement could have on all parties involved, including the kids. I desired a peaceful life filled with happiness and love. I wanted to raise my children in a home with stability and calm. Despite my desire to live differently from my parents, I had attracted the very circumstances into my life and marriage that I wanted to avoid. Of course, I now understand this is what happens when people suffer from emotional addiction, codependency, and unresolved issues.

As fate would have it, beyond the grief of divorce and loss, I would find not only the man who would be my partner in creating the very life I always dreamed of, but also the person who would help me discover my true calling and inspire me to rise to my highest potential. We met through a mutual friend, and if there is such a thing as love at first sight, I believe that is what we experienced.

On a warm spring evening, I was out with a large group of friends and family for cocktails at an outdoor restaurant. We were supposed to meet up with our mutual friend, but our friend never showed up. I looked down the street and saw my future husband walking toward me. I recognized him from a photograph on our mutual friend's Facebook page. He was wearing a white shirt and jeans and had the warmest and friendly smile I had ever seen. Has that ever happened to you — when you look at someone, and you can just feel the goodness of their heart shining through their smile? I waived at him as he made his way through crowds of people to get to our table. I was so happy to see this stranger I had never met. When he got close enough, we hugged. He sat down next to me and introduced himself to everyone as Sean. We immediately fell into an easy conversation. There was a familiarity between us that was felt by me and sensed by others at the table. When he got up to go to the bathroom, I remember someone asking, "So how long have you known this guy?"

"Ummm...as long as you. I just met him!"

Meeting him that night felt as if I had reconnected with a long-lost friend. Through the years getting to know him, about his life, his goals, his dreams...his heart and integrity so inspired me. He grew up in a middle-class family, and after his parents divorced, there were times when they didn't have much; however, he developed such a strong sense of appreciation for all that they did have. His family was and still is very close-knit. I found it so sweet that he would call his mother every Sunday and always created the time and space to have a meaningful conversation with her.

I remember shortly after we met, he had a business meeting two towns over. At the time, he lived in a large metropolitan city, and for the most part, didn't need a car since most everything was within walking distance. In this situation, most people would catch a cab, an Uber, or some other form of public transportation to their meeting. Not him. He loved to walk, often walking for miles each day just because he enjoyed being outside. On this particular day, it was HOT — we're talking one-hundred-degree-humid-Florida-summer-HOT. He mentioned that he had a lunch meeting and was going to walk there. This was about a two-hour walk. So, walk, he did, and when he arrived at the meeting, he was the first person there.

He casually mentioned this to me in conversation later in the day, and it's something that still stands out to me many years later. To me, it was a shining example of the kind of man he is. Without excuse, and despite obstacles along the way, he showed up first.

Being with someone humble, kind, compassionate, and considerate was something so inspiring to me. It ignited a dream in my heart that not only would I know true happiness, but also live to my highest potential. I believe we all have a special gift within us, and sometimes that gift is brought to light by the encouragement and love of others.

Shortly after Sean and I were married, we decided to have a child together. This was a big decision for us, as we were both in our forties and still figuring out the intricacies of blending a family. We just knew we were meant to have a child together and add to our family. Married life was interesting, with so many moving parts and changes. My mother, now an elderly widow and experiencing health challenges, lived with us at the time. My eldest daughter had moved home temporarily with her infant son, and we were both working full-time corporate careers and figuring it all out as we went. With so many people to take care of, we found ourselves living paycheck to paycheck, and with our child's pending birth, wondering where we were going to come up with an extra $1,100.00 a month for daycare. It had been nearly a decade since I had my previous child, and I was shocked at how much childcare costs had increased.

A friend of mine had suggested that I look into starting my own business, and for the life of me, I couldn't come up with an idea for one. I thought about refinishing furniture because I enjoyed doing that, but it was both time-consuming and hard work with my job and pregnancy. I was not entrepreneurial by any stretch, so trying to come up with something I'd like to do seemed nearly impossible.

Halfway through my pregnancy, Sean woke up one morning and realized that in just five months, he would have a baby to take care of. With very little energy to get through the days as it was, he panicked. We were both exhausted, and with little time left to do much outside of work, he was not feeling his best. He wanted to be able to get on the floor and play with our baby, his first biological child; however, he found it challenging to stay up past 7:00 most evenings. This was when one of the greatest pivotal moments of my life took place.

A former co-worker experienced a fantastic shift in her life by utilizing health solutions that were distributed through a direct sales model. I had no prior experience with direct sales or network marketing. After watching her transform before my eyes, I asked what she was doing because I thought my husband could benefit from whatever it was. When I found out it was direct sales, I didn't want him to do it. Even though I didn't know anything about it, I was just closed to the idea. I thought it was only another one of those "pyramid things." He wasn't of the same mindset. After extensive research and consideration, he decided to try it because he was tired of feeling tired. Within days, his energy had improved and he couldn't stop talking about how good he felt. Simply because it was there, I started using the nutrition and started feeling amazing myself, despite being pregnant with my fifth child at the age of 41.

What I started noticing was how we felt before — being tired all the time, irritable, lacking energy — was the norm for many of our peers. Was this The American Dream that everyone talked about? You work 60 hours a week to feel exhausted and live paycheck to paycheck and only have 48 hours a week to do everything you need to do so you can feel miserable on Sunday night, living your life for that big TGIF moment once a week?

It couldn't be. Or was it?

I used to talk about this with Sean, and he would encourage me to explore the business model within the direct sales company we were now part of. I thought he was crazy. Although I loved to help people, I was shy in a lot of ways and had a tremendous fear of rejection. I was not a salesperson and knew nothing about network marketing or direct sales or any type of sales for that matter. But he insisted. He poured so much belief into me because he knew that it was so much more than sales. He knew that more than anything, this was an opportunity to fulfill my life's dream of being of service to others and doing so would allow me to be in alignment with my highest potential.

The first year of being an entrepreneur was not easy. Juggling a full-time career and new baby made for some interesting times! However, I had committed to learning the skills necessary to succeed, and I believe that one commitment changed the trajectory of my life forever. Network marketing often has a bad rap. I'm sure you know at least one person who has tried their hand at a home-based business and failed. Prior to beginning my own journey into direct sales, I knew of plenty, I just didn't even know that what they did was network marketing! Many people think of it as a get rich quick opportunity. Although making a great deal of money in a short period of time IS possible, if it doesn't happen immediately, people quit before they even have a chance to succeed. I committed to giving it at least four years. I figured that if I could go to school and earn a degree in that period, I should be able to learn enough that would allow me to find success in our new endeavor.

It wasn't until our second year of business that things really began to take off. What I love so much about this profession and business model is that those who truly succeed do so by helping others find success. That was something I fell in love with when I first started, and it is something that continues to inspire me to this day. When I learned this and put it into action, our business experienced exponential growth, and along with our business, I began to grow as a person. Gone was the fear, hesitation, and self-limiting belief that I carried with me from childhood. In its place were confidence, conviction, and unwavering perseverance, knowing that I could and would achieve all my goals and dreams. And speaking of dreams, I learned how to dream again! This is something that most adults forget how to do!! Remember those hopes and dreams that used to cause butterflies in our bellies as kids? They are back again, and I'm here to tell you that if you're in a place in your life where you're not dreaming and butterflies are not dancing in your belly, you deserve to start letting go and allowing yourself the opportunity to get back to that place!

When I finally aligned with who I indeed was at my core, doing something that I truly loved to do, the world started opening up to me. All the things that I am living and experiencing today were there all along; my heart, my mind, and my eyes were just closed and didn't see them. And guess what? They are there for you, too! Your past does not define you; you can do and be anything you desire. Right here, right now is the only moment that matters. Sometimes it just takes someone lending us a little belief until we can believe in ourselves, and I believe in you!

I hope this glimpse into my life will give you the courage to do the things you've been putting off, or simply didn't believe you could do, because you can! On the other side of that fear and hesitation may just be the life of your dreams; you just have to open up your heart and your mind and your eyes to see it. It's there. It always has been. Now it's time for you to show up and live it!

"The beautiful thing about fear is when you run to it, it runs away."

~ Robin Sharma

CHAPTER SIX

---❖---

Finding Your Heart

By Matt Bruce

What Is Your Greatest Fear?

We were built, conditioned, trained, and controlled not to feel fear. This is particularly the case for men, as we are often taught to disconnect from our emotions from an early age. I have both witnessed and felt this myself. As we suppress one emotion in this life, we slowly disconnect from all of them. And in this, we are unaware that our journey has started as we slowly march towards our greatest fear.

I, too, had disconnected from my emotions. No joy! No empathy! No compassion! No love! No fear!

I was suffering on the inside, but no part of me was alive enough to express it. I was numb. I only looked for ways to disconnect from the pain. If you listened carefully, you could hear my pain. Everything was chaos inside and out because, when we disconnect from our internal emotions, they continue to fester and swirl, without control.

Are You Disconnecting?

When suppressed, fear can be all-consuming like a fire and volatile like a volcano. We are so terrified to tap into it, let alone express it. The emotion that we spend our lives running from is the very thing we collect and place in our pockets to witness at a later date and are ready to integrate in any present moment. It causes a level of pain and struggle, slowly and steadily affecting our external lives. When we find ourselves suppressing our emotions—our fears—it is much like looking into a mirror: everything is reflected back at us, anger and pain flow with no control or filter.

So, the next time you meet someone who opens his mouth and all you hear is anguish, have mercy, have compassion, have tolerance. If you pay attention, you can see a snapshot into that person's inner turmoil of emotions. That turmoil is visible in their words, the source is never the mind. The mind is just the projection of the reflection of suppressed emotions that can no longer be held or felt.

Are Your Actions From
A Place Of Love Or Fear?

In another life, I was a soldier. I spent ten years in the Australian Army with multiple deployments and time spent supporting the SAS. After my first deployment to Afghanistan, I had disconnected from my body and was slowly conditioning myself to live from a distant place in my mind. My intensive exercise routine kept me balanced, a coping mechanism for releasing my suppressed emotions in short bursts, but nothing to ease the pain.

To others, my exterior would look confident, that of a leader not afraid to back myself and not afraid to tackle any task and make it work. Yet, on the inside, I was a hollow shell of a man. I was attempting to fill a massive void that was deep inside. In conversations, relationships, work, and more, I would look to the external world to ease my mind of my biggest fear.

What Is Holding You Back?

Your body is built to feel fear. This is in our biology. Yet, as a soldier, this can be warped, controlled and influenced by our own minds. Many men that suppress emotions such as sadness have built a belief that it is not okay to feel sad. This is the biggest lie we tell ourselves. And, as we continue to lie and mislead ourselves, our minds are the only witnesses to what is truly going on inside.

Your mind is filled with thoughts of outrage for your partner, but you have disconnected from your heart. That is your conditioning; you feel safer to connect with the thoughts of heartache than with the emotion. This can be very confusing because your mind is activated but your feelings are not. Your senses start to face outward; your ears, eyes, and mouth begin to look for confirmation elsewhere. You are convinced that the story of your heartbreak is due to the external world because, once there is a separation between the heart and mind, your thoughts and actions are rooted in pain. We create a duality. This duality is then reflected in the world around us and creates separation in everything.

What Parts Of Yourself Are You Not Accepting?

As men, we may not like to admit this, but our hearts are very tender and gentle. As I said earlier, once one emotion is suppressed, the rest slowly suffer the same fate. Once we are closed, we can spend our lifetimes looking externally to find ourselves. This can be very destructive, looking for cheap thrills, people-pleasing, problem-solving, drugs, loving unwisely, overworking, or over-exercising, because the mind only knows of survival and every other moment other than the present. It seeks anything and everything to fill that void—to finally feel full.

Should we have the courage to sit within our own hearts and process our pain on its deepest levels, then we can mend the separation. This is what we refer to as an open heart. But it is not until the mind gets a shock that change will be born. When we walk down a destructive path and realize we are going against our own survival, that is when we can change our direction towards self-development in search of a better life and existence. It's often at these low points that the mind admits defeat and the desire to change our lives grows within us from a small flame to a raging fire.

Yet, still, don't be fooled. This is still survival mode programming, we are still running from our fears, just in a different direction.

Is Your Greatest Fear That You're Not Loved?

The collective mind has a deeply rooted story of not feeling loved. This story can be so deeply ingrained that it's stopping us from feeling our true worth and from realizing the untapped potential that lives inside every one of us. I believe that the mind's chronic thinking and unbalanced ways are the byproduct of our deep wounds. Our over-dominant minds are created from our deep wounds—those feelings of being unloved and unlovable. We all have them, and yet we are not all aware. This wound then projects our mental prison and causes us to activate our most deep-seated survival mechanisms.

For lifetimes, we look for wording and signs that we are loved and whole. Yet we contradict the very presence of any results we find. We deny it within ourselves and become something else. In this process, a bizarre reality is born as the mind starts to see itself as your very being, an image of you that it recreates and reinforces from the very same flawed thought process that led you to believe that you are not loved or lovable.

We are not merely facing our greatest fear; some of us are living our greatest fear every second of every day. In this, we create a story that we are not of the same love that creates the most profound harmony through every living being.

I believe we indeed are this love; we always have been and always will be. Once this is witnessed and accepted, there is no doubt that we are and always have been whole—that any other interpretation of reality was just the construct of our minds, an illusion, a program playing on repeat.

Do You Have The Courage To Die?

The death of self is a concept that many sages across the globe have spoken about. The death of the mind and the body's death can seem like a strange concept when the philosopher is still here to tell the tale. How can one be dead yet always be present to gift us this truth and the presence of his or her heart?

Because the sage has died in a particular way! He has lain down his very existence, surrendered to his greatest fear of death. The identity, the very construct of his mind, has surrendered. He has surrendered his deepest love, surrendered his deepest survival instinct, surrendered all material possessions; everything is gone. In this, the sage has surrendered his mind and reconnected to his true harmony within. He is now in perfect balance and connected with a deeper love that is omnipresent, one that is felt throughout his entire being. To receive such harmony in this life is a true gift.

Do You Have The Courage
To Explore Your Deepest Fear?

This level of surrender is very narrow. It is dark. The fear is almost omnipresent because the mind is aware of this deep surrender. The mind clutches at straws to hold on, searching for new information to make sense of what it sees. Often this can look like attempting to create labels and knowledge as a last-ditch effort to circumvent this final surrender. If you are brave enough, if you dare to walk towards your greatest fear, you may find the very truth that exists inside of you.

The true mystery of life and all its glory that lives external to our hearts is but an illusion filled with separation and duality, pain and chaos. The further we walk from our center into the world, the more chaotic our experience. We are truly connected to the center of our life force and our ability just to be. A true warrior of the heart fights real battles inside, in stillness, in his or her inner world. They confront their storm, piece by piece, moment by moment—only to witness that they are and always have been the creator of this storm. We must take ownership of our own internal projections, pain, and heartbreak, and move forward to help others face their fears.

Do You Have The Courage To Feel Real Love?

When we start to unpack our many layers, most of the objects and behaviors that we interact with daily are a cover or a mask we have formed. For me, the fear that I was unlovable was so deep within me that I ran from it instead of facing it. I had developed so many layers to hide from it. I did not have the stillness within me or in my outer world to truly understand my heart's deep pain. I was always running.

All I had known in my life was action, not able to sit down and relax. Unable to participate in a day without restless thoughts. I would cover my own fear of not being loved by falling in love—the kind of deep, hypnotizing

love to give me the closest opportunity to really feel it.
Yes, my heart would have flashes, yet I knew nothing of
true love. Because in reality, I never truly loved myself.

We can only ever be loved to the depths that we love
ourselves. Our heart is just a mirror and the world is our
reflection. To break the habits of self-loathing, you must
march, run, and sprint towards the stillness of your center
point—the quiet spot in the middle of your storm. Your
mind will attempt to stop you, but it can't. The path may
be windy, dark, and nothing close to linear, but if your
burning desire for truth is present, you can reach it. For
me, this took many years.

Are You Lying To Yourself?

My mind and ego were mirrored in very different ways.
This would manifest by not allowing me to accept who I
was. I was fake. My self-image was a projection to
protect me from the pain of my broken heart. And when
my mask was not accepted, my whole world and
perspective would come crumbling down. My mind
would do anything—and I mean anything—to never feel
that level of heartbreak again.

My mind had created layers to protect my insecurities
from being seen. My behavior and my personality were
clearly coming from a place of fear. My very center was
artificial, an act, a lie. I was deeply attached to this
identity, the very act that was causing me to lie, be
defensive, and seek validation from irrelevant or harmful
things. Every word, thought, action, and behavior kept me
trapped in this false image, this thing which did not exist.

So, nearly every activity in my life was based on lack, a problem, and a need for a solution. This is a place of always moving forward so as not to have the time and space to see my own truth. I know now that I was trying to outrun it.

If you were to interpret the world through your own mind and fear-based reality, things would look pretty crazy. Even when the external world seems insane, it is up to you to see it differently. If you are lucky enough to see this through your heart's lens, you will have a view of peace, harmony, and rest. Yet if you view this through the mind, you will see the world as chaos. The same can be said for our relationships, our careers, and all aspects of our lives. The more centered we are, the less chaos we experience. This is purely based on the fact that the more centered we are, the more we come from a place of heart, and the world and our perception around us reflect this. We are the very creator of duality.

So, if you see nothing but chaos, if you feel nothing but pain, do not project it outwards and do not run from it. Be brave, stand your ground like a warrior, and be gentle with your own heart. To sit within this stillness and find acceptance will require real warrior strength. Witnessing your pain and fears and processing through your many defense layers may feel like you're being set alight by the fire of your own emotions. Yet, in these very flames, the layers will be melted away and what remains is the most authentic version of you.

Are You Ready For Your Own Journey?

When I traveled my path of acceptance, I finally understood what devotion and trust truly mean. I knew that, should I find and follow my heart, that the pain experienced in this would be immense.

I had to face the separation between my heart and my mind, a separation which I had created through labels, masks, and judgments. Even though I was enticed into hiding from it all because of my upbringing and society's pressure, doing so went against my heart and my truth. This was the biggest betrayal to myself.

When I sat in my fear and processed it, in an instant I saw shame. I saw guilt. I saw action. I could see the circle of my actions creating the separation, as well as everything I had done to cut off my emotions. So, I sat, I waited, I softened, I felt, and I witnessed. I looked past the stories of my betrayal and my actions. And in that moment, I saw the meaning of devotion. I was totally devoted to a new way of being. I accepted a new set of rules, a unique experience, and a new level of trust was born within the depths of my inner world.

What Is Your Greatest Fear?

It's kind of funny, but when I had finally processed it all and found the new version of myself fully aligned with my heart and mind, a new fear was born. I now fear that my heart will close again one day. And I know that it will be my very own actions that might cause this to happen.

Are this fear and my initial fear the same? My actions to prevent heartbreak and pain ended up causing me pain, and only a fool would believe they could walk this earth and never be hurt. In reality, we need to continue to walk our own paths with open hearts, even with the possibility of being hurt. We need to be brave enough to be vulnerable, to walk this life in the deepest of surrender and allow our hearts to be okay. This is the way of a true warrior, to live with our hearts on our sleeves in every moment.

It's time to remove the separation between mind and heart and question the belief systems that we have formed for ourselves. This is so very important. Because with each belief we stay trapped in the mind. Yes, it is hard to imagine an empty mind, no identity, no beliefs, and no judgments, but that is the way of the warrior. To stand in the absence of it all, and yet to be fully connected to it all. No heaven, no hell, no man, no woman, no titles, no names. As a nobody once told me, "a nobody going nowhere." In this absence, our mind and separation are removed and, by default, so is our greatest fear—the lack of our own love.

How Well Do You Know Love?

Life is such a journey of love, and love is such a journey. To know something is to have wisdom. Wisdom is something that must be accessed—not through reading and not through seeing—through doing. Wisdom is something that is always there in every moment, if we are still and authentic with ourselves. We can access our fullest wisdom through love. Should you be lucky enough to know love in this life, then you know. Often our wisdom will come in the stillness in the aftermath of our action. So take this opportunity. This life was made to love.

I know that if I were on my deathbed I would have loved myself, my friends, my family, and complete strangers to my fullest potential in every moment. Wisdom understands there is never any future moment to love. Only the present moment exists for you to love fully in every interaction.

The only thing stopping you is you.
So take a breath then face your fears.

You Are Ready!

Be still. Ask the tough questions. Be brave. Choose love. Walk towards the center of your storm and your chaos will change shape. Your disorder will go from the external to internal, but it will still be felt. In the internal you will start to see the root. You will begin to see the true creation of this storm. Stillness is where our true self-worth and true identities are witnessed; the mind is the gateway, a distraction, just noise. Silence is where all of your fears melt away; they slowly dissolve to the point that they are no longer fears. As I was able to strengthen my stillness, I dared to sit in all of the fear I had suppressed from war.

As a young male, I was not allowing myself to feel fear. I had disconnected from this emotion, and I had to pay the price until I could find stillness. My inability to integrate these parts of my inner world cost me some of the loves of my life. I was broken, I was toxic, I was unaware. The fear from my past was buried so deep inside me that it blinded me. It took control of me—my own volcano, ready to erupt and change my life in so many ways.

To all of the warriors who are suppressing emotions, my heart goes out to you. I have so much compassion for you because you are not broken and everyone is only ever doing their best. You just need love, as we all do—love for yourself, and time to sit with your fear.

"Fear - Has two meanings:
Forget everything and run.
Or
Face everything and rise.
The choice is yours."

~ Zig Ziggler

CHAPTER SEVEN

❖

What Would You Do If
You Wouldn't Be Scared?

By Nicole Seeger

"What would you do if you wouldn't be scared?"

My grandmother's words still echo in my head today, 33 years after she passed away. She had always pushed me to see beyond my fear, beyond the visible and invisible enemy inside my head that tried to talk me out of things. She was my teacher and cheerleader, and to this day, her thought-provoking questions have stayed with me.

Her words came back to remind me when I started working as an international model in New York in my late teens. I was worried I wouldn't fit in with these larger-than-life famous models who filled the covers of international magazines. I kept telling myself that I was not like them, just not quite beautiful enough, skinny enough, talented enough.

When it came to it, being a model looked so glamorous and interesting: magazines, runway shows, and fame, while traveling the world — at least this is what I expected when I flew across the world to follow my dream. Still, my reality was quickly shattered when I moved into a tiny, overcrowded, filthy apartment off Park Avenue in Manhattan. Sirens roared outside my barred windows and loud screams coming from the busy streets kept me up at night. I shared the space not only with eight underage girls from all over the world but also had daily visits from cockroaches and rats. I slept with my luggage key under my pillow and put my name on every single food item I bought, knowing full well that there would be a good chance that it would be gone before I knew it.

It felt like I was a walking clothes hanger, marching from one go-see or photo shoot to another, always completely presentable with an extra pair of high heels, a sexy outfit, and nude underwear ready to go. For a while, this lifestyle proved to be somewhat exciting and interesting, especially considering I was escaping my regular life in Canada — a life where I had lost my voice and sense of self. Pleasing my family to fit in, I was desperate to prove myself and lost my health in the interim. When it was time to return home, I felt broken. I felt like a failure, not quite realizing just yet that life had other plans for me.

My grandmother's words echoed back to me over twenty years later when a rough wakeup call arrived at my doorstep, putting a threatening halt on my life and causing me to question everything.

"Mommy, are you ok?" my six-year-old daughter asked, concerned, as she found me staring at my reflection in the mirror of our 1950's Mullumbimby rental.

Two draining bags were clipped to my sports bra, halfway filled with fluid and blood. As I stood there, gathering myself, I realized that at this moment that I had the opportunity to either build or destroy my daughter's perspective on what beauty truly means. Various scenarios ran through my head; some were heart-driven and honest, some involuntarily reactive, some mean or distracting, and others were just a lie to get me out of the situation.

An internal force pushed me past my fear to stand there completely vulnerable and raw as I went with my heart and explained, "I am re-learning to really love myself. I am a little confused at the moment, and that is ok, my love."

When I decided to have my 18-year-old breast implants removed a few weeks earlier, I was everything but prepared for the rawness of this moment. The tear-jerking, bone-churning realness, as well as the unpreparedness to face the new me was as difficult as facing the unapologetic inquisitiveness of my daughter. All I wanted when I made this decision was to get my life back. I was convinced that I was a pretty tough cookie and had been dealing with a lot of pain. Still, having to go on living with 32 life-threatening symptoms covering a wide range of ailments, most of which I had never even heard of before, became a reality I wasn't ready to accept.

I felt paralyzed by yet another previously unknown disease, imbalance, disorder, or deficiency. My body had turned into a wounded and sorry mess, and my mental state was on a steady decline. I watched my children walk away from me, going about their day, playing and growing. Frequently, they would turn around in disbelief, looking at me and wondering when their Mommy would finally get better. I spent most of my days in bed fading away, forever questioning why this was happening to me. It never occurred in the moment, that, in fact, it was all happening for me.

I was stuck in a victim mentality and couldn't see the forest for the trees because I was so busy being scared. Facing those very fears would have meant I'd have to come face to face with the invisible enemy I was busy protecting myself against. Somehow, I had forgotten how important it was for me to live an authentic life full of love. Maybe I was not ready to leave behind my outdated thought forms and conditioning because I was looking on the outside for answers. I would run away, hide, or pretend that whatever was happening wasn't real, which gave me a short-lived but temporarily satisfactory sense of peace.

I wanted it all, but then again, perhaps I didn't if it meant experiencing hardship, challenge and pain. Could it possibly be that everything was conspiring in my favor and some wishes were just answered differently from others? Could it be me who felt like labeling things as good or bad?

Being uncomfortable when things were not right or people were not ok, was a truth I had taken away from challenging life situations thus far. Always trying to fix things, making them better than they looked, editing, or minimizing… I truly had it down pat. Yet, in this case, I was at a loss. I couldn't fix me. I couldn't minimize how I felt or distract myself any longer.

Everything had escalated so quickly after we started traveling. Almost one year earlier, my little family and I had given it all up: our 9-5, our comfort zone, and beautiful house with ocean view in West Vancouver; all of our worldly possessions were either sold or gifted. Little did we know we would be in for the adventure of a lifetime. To give it all up meant letting go, throwing all caution to the wind, and letting the great river of life take us along with her. When we jumped on the opportunity to restart our life, my husband Robin stood there one morning, just after he had left for work. With a palm tree in one arm and a box of personal belongings tucked under the other, he said, "I quit!"

Things became real from there on. Everything seemed to move at lightning speed, and before I knew it, our home was empty and four large suitcases were packed into a taxi that was ready to take us to the airport. We learned quickly that having no expectation of what was to come was the only way to meet this new life — to let go of the comfort of the box we had lived in up to that moment. Still, we were oblivious that what we would be embarking on would be as much of an internal journey as an external one. After all, we just wanted to be free. We wanted to grow and thrive together instead of apart and collect experiences instead of things…get to know the world. And so, we did. On June 29th, 2017, our first ticket of many took us to Japan.

Again, my grandmother's words reminded me to release the fear of the unknown and lean into the adventure.

One crazy cool experience after another, we let the rapids move us exactly where we were supposed to go. You could say we were pretty brave, never really knowing where we would end up next and often booking our next accommodation at the airport to our new destination. Many thought we were downright crazy, nuts, and irresponsible with two children under the age of ten. World-schooling our children meant giving up on the agenda to have it a particular way and let the reality of being a traveling family teach them. Surrender and patience became our new teachers. Curiosity and flexibility were closely following behind. Robin and I had never done this before, or even prepared for it; yet, it felt like a huge accomplishment, seeing our children Raphael and Aviana grow more confident, independent, and free every day.

We continuously opened our hearts and minds to what life would offer us next. Curious and adventurous, forever expanding our worldview, I felt that something kept lingering beneath the surface. Like a sleeping giant, something seemed to have followed us, and me, in particular. I couldn't quite put my finger on it yet. We had traveled through Japan, Singapore, Indonesia, Malaysia, New Zealand, and Fiji when life had suddenly become a different kind of adventure.

About seven months after our travels began, I found myself crawling on the kitchen floor of our New Zealand Airbnb, succumbing to yet another spell of extreme vertigo and nausea. Not many things made sense anymore. One doctor visit after another revealed that there was nothing wrong with me other than low iron, low B12, and some other minor deficiencies; yet my white blood cell count was abnormally high — a condition known as leukocytosis. When there is a great infection or underlying disease, our body goes into overdrive, trying to kill the enemy.

What was it I was so desperately fighting?

As I kept searching for the missing puzzle piece, a friend sent me a random article about a celebrity coming out with her story fighting Breast Implant Illness. Suddenly, it clicked. Everything fell into place as if I had finally found that missing piece of the puzzle. There were many different symptoms including Hashimoto, Lyme disease, extreme fatigue, random sensitivity to light or sound, debilitating aches and pains, bloating, and weight gain.

Could it really be true that I wasn't the only one experiencing this? I started connecting the dots when I found one Facebook support group after another, all dedicated to women suffering from Breast Implant Illness. One group had over 115,000 women sharing their stories of how their implants were poisoning their bodies and lives. A huge weight lifted off my shoulders that day. I was not alone. Others were fighting this seemingly invisible enemy, too. The only way to get better would mean surgically removing the implants and waving my perfectly perky 34D's goodbye, which meant traveling to Australia to have this complicated surgery.

For all these years, my breasts had been my friend, my safety net, my solution to feeling better about myself. My body had always been out of proportion, or so I felt. My breasts distracted me from feeling lesser than and not good enough. They accompanied me through major life transitions and helped me feel whole. The prospect of removing them came with a truckload of unresolved wounds that rushed to find me with a vengeance. As I had always been aware of the body-mind connection, I was ready to dig deeper. What would I find beneath the layers of my self-imposed prison?

After years of self-developmental work, there was a deep shadow searching to reveal unhealed trauma, knowing that this journey would go on as long as I would live. It looked like I had hit a roadblock. Then, a flashback hit. Vivid as could be, I suddenly remembered my initiation into the North American Native Tribe that changed my life. I always felt alone and different, not fitting in or belonging and always striving to make sense of it all. During a spiritual retreat, I was invited to assist at Mount Shasta in California a couple of years earlier. I went through a dark spell of feeling wholly unwanted and invisible. It left me feeling utterly alone in the world, and although I was surrounded by beautiful people who loved and supported my journey, I couldn't shake the feeling of not fitting in...again.

Suddenly I found myself amidst a dense smoke cloud of burning sage, frankincense, and sweetgrass, which are used to clear negative energies and ward off evil spirits. At the same time, a ceremony began — a ceremony for me. I felt the enormous weight of the button blanket on my shoulders, which reminded me of the recurring heaviness I was experiencing when I felt unlovable or not good enough. Only this time, I was wrapped up in a ceremonial piece, symbolizing the duties, rights, and privileges of the Tahltan Clan members of Northern British Columbia, a small tribe close to the Alaskan Border. Song, drums, and spoken word broke out around me when I felt pulled into a powerful shift, a change in trajectory for my life. Time seemed to stand still as the initiation and ceremony commenced, and I was made part of the clan as a crow, the one that gives light to Mother Earth.

The tribe knew a thing or two about metamorphosis and transformation, and the connectedness of all was tangible in the energy around me. How serendipitous to have found a place for my aching heart with a tribe like that. An elder handed me her carved silver bracelet as a gift to officially welcome me into her clan.

With the roadblocks dissolving in front of my eyes and my grandmother's voice reminding me again of the power and willingness to change, I felt ready. I knew the time had come to renew my lease on life. As I was waiting to get prepped for the last-minute operation to get my implants removed, tears of grief and disbelief rolled down my cheeks, which created a small puddle on the crispy blue liner beneath me. I was no longer grieving for my breasts, which would be taken from me today; this time, I was grieving for my dad.

I had received a call from his girlfriend in Germany informing me that he had been in and out of the hospital, in and out of consciousness, and in rough shape.

"He only has a couple of days left," she said. "He is drifting further and further away. You better come now if you want to say goodbye."

The travel back to Germany from Australia meant traveling for 30 hours — something I would not even think twice about if it meant being able to say goodbye to my dying father. The doctors warned me not to fly. "It is you or your dad…you'll have to make that choice."

I'll never forget the sharp pain that pierced my heart at that moment. This would truly have to be the biggest act of self-love I would ever have to face, to let myself be more important than someone else, which happened to be my dad. I knew I had work to do in that area, but all of this through the cold reality of not being able to say goodbye and see him one more time was overwhelming.

"You must be joking!" I argued with the universe. "This is unacceptable." But my body didn't lie. She told me exactly what to do. I said my last goodbye to my father over the phone.

While his silent stutter still echoes in my soul today and etches deep grief into my heart, so does his constant reaffirming nudge that I come first. He always reminded me that whenever life would get tough and the world would seem unfair, he would be the one standing right behind me to lean and fall back on. He wanted me to take good care of myself. He knew.

He knew that my life wasn't always easy — that from the time he had separated from my mom, things would get foggy and confusing. He knew how stubborn and determined I could be. He was also very aware that I had learned to please everyone else before looking after my own needs. Pleasing meant safety, and safety was a hot commodity when growing up in a dysfunctional family. Putting myself last meant less confrontation and more peace.

As the anesthesiologist rolled my stretcher into the operating room, or as Aussies call it, the theatre, it must have been evident that I was having a hard time.

"What do you need?" a gentle voice with an equally soft pair of eyes carefully inquired.

Even more tears streamed down my face and left me sobbing as the last couple of months and years suddenly appeared a whole lot more realistic than ever before.

"My dad," I replied.

As I struggled to breathe through the tears, I could feel his sensitivity for my case.

"I am sure he is with you," the anesthesiologist said.

"Yes, he is."

As my mind settled and my body relaxed into the sedation, there he was. A faint, yet deeply recognizable scent, and feeling his presence soothed my soul. My dad stood there right next to me, holding my hand.

"I am so proud of you for looking after yourself first. This will be the doorway to your new life. You'll see."

His words echoed and stayed with me until I drifted off.

Looking down at my now flat chest with draining bags dangling, I took a deep breath, welcoming it all: the confusion, discomfort, and awkwardness that come with inhabiting a brand-new form. Something deeply touching and innocent returned home at that moment. It reminded me that no one and nothing on the outside could make me feel better about myself. That wholeness was an inside job and a journey to be taken as an adventurous ride.

With this profound insight, my time hiding behind self-imposed masks of insecurity and safety was left behind. No more editing or minimizing the real me. I left behind years of striving for perfection, abusing and punishing my body to the point of anorexia. I was working in unforgiving industries where an overly skinny and fading physique was just about good enough. The people who told me I needed bigger breasts to fit in flashed in front of my eyes. The modeling and film industry had left their mark, a deep fold that eventually brought me back home to me.

As my daughter curiously took in my new look, touching my draining bags and flat chest, she proudly looked up to me in a way that reflected back to me that inner knowing that the choice I had made was the right one.

"You know, Mommy, you are beautiful just the way you are."

My eyes filled with tears of gratitude. The rites of passage that I just passed through suddenly reached through me, to my daughter, and what seemed through to generations yet to come.

I was made witness to the unraveling of all the societal and ancestral conditioning of perfection and not–good-enoughness that I had been part of for so long. With my dad's visit in the operating room still as vividly alive as ever, little did I know that this would be the steppingstone to a whole new expression of me.

A few months later, my little family and I found ourselves settling on Bali, the Island of Gods. After all our plans to go to Europe or Hawaii had failed for a year, we realized that life again had something different planned for us. Arriving on this powerful island in the middle of the Indonesian Archipelago sent shivers down my spine and tears down my face. I knew I had come home: home to the part of me that was ready to be fully seen as me, without editing or justification, and home to possibilities of wonder and excitement. The softness and welcoming energy of the land, people, and spirits of this place were undeniable.

Wherever we went, we were welcomed with open arms and bright smiles. It was never difficult to find accommodations, and our world-schooling adventures seemed to have come to an end when the option came up to join a beautiful school that aligned with our morals and indeed served our children. Our soul family grew quicker than we could have asked for with inspiring humans entering our lives. What a welcoming change after spending our life searching for fitting in somehow, somewhere.

It was not a long after that I was truly asked to step up into a whole new role as a guide and spiritual leader for women who were ready to ignite their own light and empowering them to find their unique, authentic expression, claiming their power and strength. What now feels like throwing many lifetimes into one, I was often challenged in my belief that I wasn't ready, that I still had to learn to be in front of others, that I was not good enough. Comparison and jealousy still snuck in, but so did my grandmother's voice asking,

"What would you do if you wouldn't be scared?"

It became more and more obvious that I was being asked to trust. With every circle I held, every retreat I facilitated, and every event I ran, I became accustomed to the fact that I was born for this…that this journey has taken me far and wide, reminding me to come home to myself. Through facing my fears, I was able to find my voice after all.

"Expose yourself to your deepest fear. After that... you are free."

~ Jim Morrison

CHAPTER EIGHT

---◆---

The End of The Fucking World

By Carol Williams

I dedicate this chapter to my dear friend Yvonne, whom we lost during the writing of this chapter. She was one of my greatest teachers.

The year is 2020 and the shit has hit the fan.

A global pandemic has killed millions within a matter of months, leaving the living scared and isolated. There are protests worldwide, with long-overdue attention being drawn to racism, sexual harassment, and inequality worldwide. #BLM #MeToo #LoveWins

We have world leaders (one in particular) who are off-the-charts crazy and devastating environmental disasters, from fires to floods. Conspiracy theories and corruption are coming to light, and oh yeah, don't forget the killer hornets!

What The Actual F…!

It's safe to say there's good reason to feel off-center when things big or small happen outside of our control. Perhaps even fearful. The good news is, if you're reading this, the world has not ended!

Armageddon, Or Life As We Knew It

No joke: I believed the end of the world was just around the corner for years. I was raised a Jehovah's Witness and have spent a great deal of my life living in fear of Armageddon.

Most people will never experience such an extreme, but periodically things happen which can bring up fear and anxiety. Depending on your upbringing and support system, it affects some people more frequently and intensely than others. It can even feel like it's the end of the world - your world.

Listening only to the messages in the media makes it worse. For some reason, fear-based messaging sells, and we are bombarded with it every day. But, in those moments, we tend to forget (and need to remember) that scary, uncertain events will continue to come and go in our lives. Come rain, come shine. This is the polarity of life. It may sound clichéd, but the fact is there can be no light without darkness. In this most recent coronavirus crisis, many people have lost their jobs, parents have taken over the role of teachers, relationships have suffered, and many feel alone. Even worse, some have lost friends and family. Life will never be the same.

Life truly SUCKS sometimes, but what gets me is how easily we allow fear to continue to take charge. Why do we do this to ourselves? Perhaps I've just gotten immune after living so long with the fear that "THIS COULD BE IT"! But seriously, this is no way to live.

When the Corona shit hit the fan and people were freaking out, I realized that the time and energy I had invested in healing my past paid off. During this period, I noticed a shift in how I dealt with it emotionally. Instead of fear, I felt empowered. Instead of numb, I felt motivated. It gave me the extra incentive to get out of my own comfort zone and share my experiences to help others conquer their fears. Writing this chapter was one of the ways, but believe me, this was scary for me.

Many people have suffered far more significantly than I could ever imagine. Yet, many of these people have gone beyond surviving, to thriving, and living fulfilled lives. You can too.

In this chapter, I'll share some very personal stories that will unquestionably result in losing the last remnants of my immediate family. Through my story and sharing my transformation, I hope to inspire you into action, despite your fear, to take your next step toward a life of joy and know you're not alone.

In The Beginning

My mom was a feisty Californian girl with hair down to her butt who came from a very Christian family. Dad was a rough but charming 18-year-old Navy dude from New Jersey. The whole thing was very "West Side Story."

My parents forged my mother's birth certificate so that in 1957 they could get married. And a year later, I came along... My mom was 16!

When I was three, my baby brother died from a hole in his heart. Looking back, I can feel the grief, hopelessness, and loneliness my parents must have felt. They were just kids with not a lot of life experience and very little support.

My grandmother, who I loved with all my heart, was a hard-ass. Her reaction when my brother died was simply, "Jesus needed another angel."

There were no support groups or books to help them back then, and therapy was too expensive. It doesn't surprise me that my parents turned elsewhere for understanding.

Enter The Promise Of Paradise

Our next-door neighbors were Jehovah's Witnesses (J.W.'s) and gave my distraught father a different answer. One day, he would be reunited with his baby boy. It was precisely what he needed to hear. The promise of Paradise!

Unfortunately, my father was bipolar and I was terrified of him. Even after him finding hope and support with his newfound community, he was extremely volatile.

I remember him beating my mom when she was cowered down on the floor, crying, and I was jumping on his back to help her. I was only five years old. Mom didn't want to become a J.W., but eventually, she gave in and my father won. Even my gram said that mom should stay with him because it was safer to stay than to go. He would probably kill us. Thanks for the help, gram (not).

When I was 15 years old, I ran away from home because I was afraid that my dad would find out that I'd skipped school and there would be hell to pay. Two days later, I went home because I felt guilty for leaving my mom, and honestly, where else was I going to go?

To be allowed back in the congregation, I was forced to go before the three 'elders' and tell them what I had done in great detail (kind of pervy if you ask me) and repent. When I refused, they disassociated me from the congregation. I was accused of committing gross sins, which made me unclean — just W.O.W. I can hardly believe it myself as I type this.

J.W.'s defend the practice of shunning those who "promote false teaching," claiming such individuals must be quarantined to prevent the spread of their "spiritual infection." I was a walking venereal disease! L.O.L.! Your 'trespassing,' aka SINS, are also announced to the congregation as a warning to the rest.

As a young girl, though, I was still forced to go to the bible meetings three times a week, though no one would speak or even look at me. Since we lived in the isolated hills of West Virginia, I experienced a literal version of quarantine. This was torture. For my sanity, I had no other choice than to conform; otherwise, I'd suffer even longer in forced isolation. So I submitted or at least played the part. Like a good girl, I sat through all the bible meetings at home, did the walk of shame 3x a week at the meetings where no one would even look in my direction, and finally, I repented. Yeah, right. I was only sorry I had to follow their rules.

Humor is one of the main things that helped me survive. If I could make my mom laugh, I was super happy. It turned out to be one of the most effective state-changing tools used by coaches worldwide (including myself) and remains to this day my #1 Beauty secret.

Losing Everything

In my world, questioning any of the rules was not done.

I was raised to believe that the end of the world was coming, and if I didn't do as I was told, I would be destroyed. Consider my young brain 'washed.' I had to be extremely careful because I was told that even thinking something 'bad' was the same as doing it and Jehovah would know.

As a girl in that community, it was clear that I was to be seen and not heard. Education and extra-curricular activities, like sports or dance, were a waste of time and even dangerous because "bad associations spoil useful habits" - 1 Corinthians 15:33. Boy, was that ever rammed into my brain! After 40 years of not having even touched a bible, I still remember the warning! LORDY LORDY.

My father even made me stop going to school entirely when I turned 16 because there were too many "worldly people." Learning how to support yourself, manage finances, or learn a trade? HUH, WHY? Women were there to serve their God, husbands, community, and be a good mom. Pretty much in that order.

When I was 17, my best option, and the only way out, was to marry my best friend, a J.W. boy.

One and a half years later, I was utterly miserable and the pressure was building to start a family. I knew that I could no longer stay, so I left – with no money, education, or job, hoping to find a better life or at least one that was my own.

When my dad found out, he let me know (according to the rules) that if I didn't go back, I would never see him, my mother, or my brothers, ever again. I will always remember that day. My heart was broken. It was a primal sort of pain. I remember howling like an animal that had been shot but was not yet dead.

Gram only told me to stop crying. I was lost and had no idea who I was or how I was going to survive.

Losing Your Identity

The overwhelming suffocation of my upbringing and the stress of my situation created so much fear in me. Only years later did I dare to type "J.E.H.O.V.A.H.S. W.I.T.N.E.S.S." into the Yahoo search bar (yes, I'm that old, haha); I was shocked to learn that there were so many stories like mine.

Nonetheless, I was still living with the fear that questioning the establishment would be the final nail in my coffin, and I would become an apostate. An apostate is any baptized J.W. who openly disagrees with or speaks out against the J.W. religion. Apostates are considered dangerous "followers of Satan" and are therefore shunned.

Spoken or unspoken, nothing feels more painful and threatening than rejection. Human beings are pack animals and need the approval of their tribe for reasons that helped ensure our survival way back. It's in our genetic makeup to need other humans. We need Love and Connection.

By the way, it's not only your family who can make you feel this way. Friends, neighbors, co-workers, political cronies, church-members, fellow drug addicts, yogis, CrossFit crew, book club members, vegan buddies, activists, or sneezers in corona times... God forbid you to do the last! Oh, the looks you get these days if you have hay fever! Where was I again? Right: any person or group can turn away from an individual who dares to ascend beyond what is expected or 'allowed.'

Our tribes tell us who we are, what to believe, and sometimes – like in my case – what you can do, and what to think.

Each group has its own set of guidelines or commandments and we learn these at a very young age. Our parents or caregivers teach us specific rules, habits, morals, and standards. This is how we do things here.

You know the kind of rules. Brush your teeth before bed, close your mouth when you chew, go to church every Sunday, say a prayer before meals, or shake hands when saying hello (not doing that anymore!).

But in some communities, like the J.W.s, there are other, more ominous rules: Never speak unless spoken to. Children should be seen and not heard. A woman's place is in the home—no sex before marriage. Homosexuality is a sin. Whatever the situation, it was made very clear to you that to remain safe and accepted within the family, you must follow these rules.

Perhaps while growing up, you found that some of the rules felt right to you, or you enjoyed having this sense of structure. If so, I'm happy for you, especially if you get your ticket to Paradise at the end of it all.

But maybe along the way, you started to question some of what you were told (or, like me, all of it).

- You wanted to go to college but were told that formal education is not necessary.
- You wanted a career, but were told that girls are supposed to become full-time mothers.
- You wanted to love the world with a more open heart, but you were taught to be suspicious of strangers.
- You happen to be gay, but your church considers homosexuality to be a cardinal sin.

Our Way or The Highway

Maybe as you grew older, you found that your own values, morals, and aspirations were different from the ones that you were taught.

Maybe like me, you realized that you didn't WANT to follow in your family's footsteps.

Or maybe you decided to separate from what you were told and choose your own path. Perhaps you found new people who felt more like family than your own.

If you were lucky, your family remained your biggest cheerleaders, celebrating your differences and rejoicing in your happiness. If so, bless their hearts.

But my guess is, if you're reading this, your family wasn't OK with at least some of your choices. And if so, the stakes are always the same: our way or the highway.

Daring to follow your own path could result in disappointing people, being shamed, made to feel guilty, or even completely abandoned. In my case, I was made to feel responsible for the pain my mom felt when I left, and believe me, leaving her behind was the hardest thing I've ever done. She was my best friend. Shame and rejection are capable of ruining lives. It's even been established to cause psychological damage (like P.T.S.D.) and has been categorized as torture. Living with just the fear of rejection can keep you in a constant state of inflammation, anxiety, unease, and perhaps down the line, even disease. Regardless, it'll prevent you from showing yourself to the world, contributing your unique gifts, and being the person you long to be.

Reaching Out

At the start of the Corona crisis, I decided to reach out to different online ex-Jehovah's Witness groups. This time it would be to support those who had gone through similar things as myself, and I became a mentor — seeing the number of new members joining every week stunned me.

These are some very courageous people or people who were just so unhappy they couldn't keep living in this religious community. They had decided to leave and join a support group, but most were extremely cautious in asking for help and even using their real names. All of it gave me an overwhelming sense of déjà vu.

There were stories of repression, domestic and sexual abuse, bullying, or childhood neglect. Perpetrators were protected time and time again; often, the victims were blamed, even young children. For example, if your husband was beating you, you were told to try harder to make him happy. Are you kidding me?!

Once having left the only community they'd ever known the helplessness set in, as well as experiencing a complete loss of identity. Who am I? How on earth will I navigate this new world? Many had developed trust issues and trouble making close friends or having intimate relationships, resulting in depression and loneliness.

But it's not just people who come from enclosed communities that can feel this way. People from all walks of life often find themselves stuck and not knowing how to move forward. People in abusive relationships, going through a divorce, losing their livelihood, going through sickness, having been raised in a dysfunctional family, and other situations can make you feel insignificant or insecure. Even a happy time like becoming a new mom or moving to a new country can bring up a lot.

But if there's one thing I've learned, it's that fear is not all bad and can be a powerful force for positive change.

Fear. Friend or Foe?

Several years ago, while I was visiting my favorite place in Northern California, I was invited to go paragliding at the very last minute. This was NOT one of the things on my bucket list, as I am a great fan of keeping my feet on solid ground at all times. In other words, I was scared shitless.

Since it was one of my YES days, I decided to embrace my fear and do it anyway. WELL, WELL... what an adventure it was. After going through the do's and don'ts, I was told all I needed to do was run off the edge of a cliff with a man on my ass with a huge kite above. Great...

I went full speed ahead and, at the worst possible moment on the edge of the cliff, froze! Not one of my finer moments... Lucky for me, I had a very experienced instructor who literally rammed me from behind multiple times, pushing me over the edge, and heroically saving us from plummeting to our deaths. It's safe to say when we were finally up in the air, he was NOT amused and I was not having fun!

The textbook definition of fear is an unpleasant emotion caused by the real or perceived threat of danger, pain or harm, anxiety, and loss of courage.

As my little story points out perfectly, fear is one the most paralyzing and debilitating states you can be in. It puts your system into freeze, flight, or fight mode – a form of self-protection.

I didn't want to die, so I froze. My instructor friend didn't want to die either and went into debatably fight, then flight – thank god! These are very natural reactions and perfectly healthy when necessary, and everybody reacts differently to different life events.

Have you ever been through something similar? Living with lots of stress or fear over a more extended period is another story. Chronic anxiety continuously floods the body with stress hormones. It can lead to hormonal imbalance and burnout, leading to devastating effects on pretty much all our bodily processes and mental health.

Since our thoughts and emotions affect our physical and emotional health, investigating our fears can teach us a great deal about ourselves. The process helps us understand how fear affects our lives and can motivate us to make positive changes.

Fear can be a great advisor, but we all know that most of the things we worry about never happen!

"Today Is The Tomorrow You Worried About Yesterday"

That being said, fear can keep us safe, so when needed, we can respond accordingly. There's nothing wrong with having an emergency plan in the event of a fire or earthquake, or learning how to protect your family's health and finances.

In the end, one of my life's lessons is that where focus goes the energy flows. As in the serenity pray we need to learn to embrace the things we cannot change, the courage to change the things we can and wisdom to know the difference. While also realizing fear is not always bad.

So the million-dollar question is... will you allow fear to be your friend or foe?

Moving Beyond Fear

Before we can change anything, the first step is always awareness because you can't change what you don't recognize. A beneficial exercise is to go back to your list of New Year's resolutions from last year or the year before. If you're like me, you probably had some pretty cool things on your list. If you're like the vast majority, you never got around to doing most (or any) of them.

You're not the only one that didn't do it. We all didn't do it!

Not only did we NOT do it, but we also gave ourselves damn good REASONS why it wasn't possible. And in our minds, those reasons make a lot of sense.

"It wasn't the right time…"
"I didn't have enough money…"
"I didn't know where to start…"
"I had no one to help me…"

Cue the sad sound effects.

So the question is, what was REALLY holding you back?

You already know the answer: we were freaking scared!

We're scared of doing the hard work. That our lives would change, that this comfort level we've grown accustomed to, even if it pisses us off, will be shattered. We're scared that we won't recognize ourselves anymore. That other people might judge us or maybe start expecting more of us. What if we won't have all of the answers? We're scared that we may fail and embarrass ourselves, or that we may make the wrong choices. We're even scared that something beautiful might develop and we won't know how to handle it.

Of course, the fear of failure had to make it to the list. The majority of people fear failure, and that is OK. However, what the practice has proved is that there is no success without failure.

Fear isn't limited to this. It can also be the fear of being alone. The fear of losing family, sickness and death, relationships failing, or your children hate you—fear of not having enough money and being able to support yourself or fear being judged. The fear of public speaking is known to be as debilitating as the fear of death. What about the fear of writing a chapter in a book!

It repeatedly happens that people wait until they actually get sick, go bankrupt or end up getting a divorce before taking themselves seriously. But, I've seen firsthand how fear can also be turned into a positive and powerful motivator for Personal Growth.

I like to equate fear with courage walking. It's like a muscle. We learn to be brave when life sucks, and we confront our fears.

So, how do we embrace fear and move on?

Finding The Silver Lining

People are afraid to leave their comfort zone. One of the basic human needs is to have certainty. Whatever is outside of this is bound to be uncomfortable, so people tend to avoid it by default. If you get to the point where you start getting accustomed to that feeling of uncertainty, more opportunities will arise...

Self-doubt kills more dreams than fear ever has. So how do we move on from fear?

All it takes is a massive and decisive action...

Think of all the other people who have overcome significant challenges that have gone to do incredible things with their lives despite the fear. It's like finding a silver lining.

Let's look at my friend Yvonne, to whom I dedicated this chapter. Out of the blue, she went from a vibrant, healthy woman living an extraordinary life to waking up with locked-in syndrome, entirely dependent overnight. She was unable to move anything except to blink her eyes.

She had every reason to be afraid. She had lost total control of everything around her. Her life was over as she knew it, but she moved on, accepting the things she could change and focused on the good. She embraced laughter.

Even though she couldn't move or speak, she learned how to get what she needed and never gave up.

Tips To Expertly Complete Your Next Steps

As we get older, you might discover old patterns that have been running the show.

One of the most powerful tools that helped me to accept my past is called a family constellation or systemic therapy. This approach is designed to address limiting beliefs or destructive patterns in your life, such as relationship problems, addictions, or just general unhappiness that often has roots in our family history. It can bring to light that which is sometimes unspoken, but without blame.

Naturally, there are things you can do to continue your journey of personal development and healing. I've found helping me journaling to express and release my feelings, but here's the kicker – after writing, I tear it up or even burn it.

Another great tool is a Buddha board. It is designed to help you learn to live in the moment (mindfulness). You simply write on the surface with water, and your creation or a word like FEAR will come to life. As the water slowly evaporates, your text or art will magically disappear, leaving you with a clean slate, ready to create a whole new masterpiece.

Daily meditation, yoga, or mindfulness are scientifically proven to reduce stress and anxiety and control breathing exercises. There are some fun free apps you can download on your mobile device to help remind you.

Please limit your exposure to negative news and start to enjoy good news sources. This is such an essential part of your own self-care. It's also vital to begin reducing the amount of stress in your life and getting enough sleep.

One of the best things that have supported my own growth is using plant medicine, and essential oils for emotional wellness. I use high-grade essential oils, which have proven to help your moods and reduce stress and anxiety. Aromatherapy is one of the quickest ways to change your state of mind if you are off-balance. Lavender is well known for its relaxing properties, lemon or wild orange are happy and uplifting, tea-tree or Melaleuca can be used for energetic cleansing, and black spruce is good for grounding and stabilizing.

Another thing you can do is to ask yourself: What is the worst that could happen? Play it out. Could I survive it? What is the best that could happen? Would I or others benefit from it? Are there downsides to remaining where I am? What is holding me back?

You can also use affirmations and visualizations to improve your confidence in moving forward. Repeating sentences like, "I am brave. I can do this. I am powerful." Your mindset and the power of your words internally and externally affect you. Our thoughts are like food. Eat healthy to be healthy. Think happy to be happy.

You can start building your confidence muscle by doing things regularly that scares you. A few personal examples that have pushed me way out of my comfort zone: Firewalking, which is walking over red hot coals with bare feet while chanting "Cool moss, cool moss, cool moss," (don't try this at home kids!), going paragliding (although never again for me!), and public speaking (which is way up there on the fear pyramid right next to the fear of dying)!

All of these are calculated risks with no guarantees. But life begins at the end of your comfort zone! Like world-class athletes and successful entrepreneurs, some of the most inspirational people have failed more than they have succeeded. So go FAIL A LOT. Celebrate each time you try, with a smile on your face, because it's bringing you closer to success. This is the path to continued lifelong growth.

Don't Go It Alone

If there's one thing I've learned in my 61 years on this planet, you can't do it all alone, nor do you have to. I sure wish I had learned this earlier in life. It would have saved a lot of time, money and heartache. We all need help throughout our lives and can benefit significantly from support and a strong community during crisis and difficulty.

So please, no matter where you are in your life, things may be particularly awful and it may even feel like your world has come to an end, I encourage you to find a professional coach or therapist you feel connected with. If my voice speaks to you, I invite you to reach out, book a free clarity call, or join my like-minded international community of like-minded individuals.

It's NEVER too late. Every day we have a new chance to start again. It's important to remember that small, consistent steps will lead to remarkable results.

You are brave. You are courageous. You are important. Most importantly, you are enough and have everything you need inside of you already. Sometimes we just need someone else to shine a light so you can see it yourself.

"Always go with the choice that scares you the most, because that's the one that is going to require the most from you."

~ Caroline Myss

CHAPTER NINE

---❖---

Finding Home Within

By Nicolas Perrin

I t was touch down! As the wheels of the plane came to a screeching halt at Sydney Airport, Josh and I took a big breath in recognition of a new chapter beginning. We had just been on a successful tour to Los Angeles and San Francisco, supporting an inspirational speaker as he shared his message about accessing intuition and following one's inner knowing. Catching an overnight flight, we arrived early in the morning into Sydney during winter. The air was crisp and clear, a sharp contrast to the warmth of the West Coast of the United States.

My body and mind felt a bit discombobulated with the ninja-like shifting from summer to winter. We hurriedly made our way to my home in Alexandria to freshen up before darting off to the iconic Bondi Beach office. Upon arriving at the office, we were greeted by a frazzled Ralph who was looking at his clock, saying, "You're late!" I could feel a fiery energy bubble up from my belly. My jaw tightened and I noticed a level of irritation ring through the cells of my body. I took a breath and quietly told myself, "All is well. Just let it go!"

I sat down at my desk to prepare for another full day. I was handling a million and one things, from event management to coaching relationships and everything in between. I looked at my to-do list and began sensing which items required my urgent attention. Moments later, a strange cold feeling flowed through my body, like the venom of a snake bite slowly traversing through my veins.

My body began to freeze and it felt like someone had pulled a plug from underneath me and my energy was slowly draining, like the water spiraling out of a bathtub. The marketing manager, Jackson, squinted over in my direction and casually smirked, "It looks like your days here are numbered!"

I nervously smiled and said that everything was okay. I told him that I was adjusting to the jetlag and finding my feet again. As the day progressed, I became aware of a subtle sense of awkwardness in my body. I could feel something energetically was off kilter, yet my mind had no clarity on what was unfolding. I sensed that something was about to explode, shake, and shift in my life.

A week passed and life appeared to be business as usual. The only indication of imminent change was that I'd begun to dream that my life was becoming radically different. I saw myself traveling more, working for myself and radiating a sense of confidence and power. Up to this point in my life, I had always been employed, either by a corporation or business.

At the end of 2010, I had left my corporate job and took a fifty percent pay cut to support Ralph with the running of his events business. I'd accepted this opportunity to align my energy into a career that felt congruent with my heart and values. I no longer wanted to give my time and energy in exchange for a predictable paycheck that supported the experience of a monotonous, boring life. I wanted to feel like I was making a difference to others and the world. I decided to work for an organization where my values were aligned with the vision of the business.

Upon leaving the corporate world, I had worked in this dynamic inspirational speaker's business for eighteen months. I was grateful to have learned an enormous amount during the deep-dive immersion. My skillsets had diversified significantly compared to the super niched automatic processes I had acquired in my corporate career.

But at the end of this particular week, a team meeting was arranged. Ralph said that he had been receiving nagging intuitive insights during his meditations. It wasn't uncommon for Ralph to receive visions and to make radical choices that required a pivot and directional change in the business. He began the meeting by saying, "I am receiving an intuitive hunch that a member of the team will be leaving imminently." Everyone looked at each other in a combination of shock and curiosity. We decided to go around the table and allow each member to share what he or she was feeling in the moment. Everyone on the team started to place a hunch as to who they thought was going to be leaving. As we went around the table, located in a clinical white meeting room, the energy circulating was a combination of tension, excitement, intrigue, and anxiety.

We had almost gone completely around the circle when it was my turn. I opened my mouth and paused. I felt a rush of energy move through my body, and I boldly and confidently shared that the person leaving was me. Everyone looked rather shocked, as I wasn't the predictable guess. I said, "I feel it's time to step out into the world, to spread my wings and be independent." Tension had been building over the previous four months. I was feeling undervalued in the business and had been in negotiations to have a pay rise. Perhaps something deep within me was stirring and creating expansion and change.

The curious part was that I didn't have clarity on what the change would be or look like. It felt like another part of me was speaking. For a moment, I felt gentle confidence and excitement in my heart. I was sharing from the place of possibility and deep inner knowing. Up to that point in time, I had been referred to as "the man behind the man." My role had been one of support and implementation, to ground Ralph's dreams and make them real in the world.

I received a flashback from three months earlier. I was managing the weekend events in Sydney, and in the middle of the seminar, a woman came up to the table where I was overseeing all the book and product sales. She looked me in the eye and said, "You should be up on that stage speaking." It was one of those bizarre moments that did not make any sense. I shook my head and said I was happy supporting Ralph's business and the vital message he was spreading out into the world.

Within seventy-two hours of the decision to leave the inspirational business, to my shock and surprise, I had completed a full handover of my role. At the time, my assistant stepped into the management role, and we hired another person to take on the business's events management side. My ego had originally thought I would have one month to figure things out, but, no, Ralph wanted the transition to be swift and fast. No mucking about! Everything had unfolded so fast. I was sitting out on the southern end of Bondi Beach starring into the distance where the ocean and sky meet and wondering what had just happened. I felt an aliveness in my body as the security blankets had been violently shaken off me.

The gentle confidence and excitement that I had felt a few days earlier had shifted into anxiety and worry. I felt concerned about how I would move forward. I had never run my own business, and I had only been on my healing path since 2006. I had limited experience in supporting others on their paths of healing and self-realization.

Up to this point, I had run a few workshops and one-on-one healing sessions, supporting friends and colleagues for free or on a donation basis. I could feel the creative tension building in my inner world. My mind was concerned about how I was going to bridge myself into a new reality of possibility. When I dropped into my heart and quietened my mind, a voice and inner knowing spoke: "It's time to begin your own work! The time to step into the unknown is now. You will be supported if you commit to this path." I took a breath, and I said YES within my heart.

The next six months was the baptism by fire! I went through multiple initiations that challenged me relentlessly. I had never felt this level of fear, worry, and anxiety before. I had lived a relatively predictable life with many invisible safety blankets. Now I was truly jumping into the fire of the unknown. What was most scary was that none of this had been planned. It felt like it was orchestrated from another level of reality and I was a player in a greater game unfolding of its own accord.

I started to experience paradoxical fears. I felt a sense of relief that I didn't have to be so strict about waking up in the mornings out of fear of being late and having penalties imposed by the boss.

Then, moments later, another thought would float into my mind, which was, "Now that I don't have the pressure of being on time, what if I lay in bed and don't do anything?" The fear of running out of money or not being able to pay the bills and the rent created a need for urgent action. It felt like I was sandwiched between two different polarities of frantic action vs. analysis paralysis.

I asked myself, "What is it I need to learn so that I can pass through this challenging time?" The answer that emerged was, "Learn to master your mind and emotions and be a pillar of light and love. No matter what is happening in your world, nothing will shake, move, or ruffle you." This felt like I was being initiated into becoming a superhero. I didn't see myself as anyone special, as I had lived a relatively low-key life up to this point. I tended to blend in, observe life, and passively engage where it felt safe and secure.

I started to do research, trainings, and work with mentors to help me become unwavering within myself. I will now share some of the most important realizations that significantly supported me in moving through the baptism of fire.

Fear is my own life force energy that is being filtered through belief systems in my mind. A belief system is a thought pattern that is fully accepted to be true. Belief systems are important because they are the mechanisms through which reality is created. Belief systems can be negative or positive. Negative beliefs are restrictive, limiting, isolating, and containing. Positive belief systems are expansive and inclusive, and they align to our soul's true nature.

It's like the architectural blueprint of a building. It determines what is possible and what is not possible. Belief systems have a built-in mechanism of reinforcing themselves over and over again. Aligning to any particular belief system will cause you to naturally feel that this one choice is true, and everything else feels false. Humans in the course of history have fought and died under the guise of belief systems, be they religious, political, economic, or social.

This helped me to realize that if I am experiencing a situation or event with fear, then I am holding onto a belief system that creates a fear-based response. The actual event or situation is inherently neutral. The meaning that I am giving through the belief system is what creates the experience for me through my perception of filtered reality.

A simple analogy to demonstrate this point is to consider public speaking. For many people, speaking in front of a group creates enormous fear, anxiety, self-doubt, and worry. For other people, speaking in front of a group creates joy, happiness, fulfillment, and excitement.

A person who experiences fear is more than likely aligning with belief systems that define public speaking in one or more of the following ways.

"I am going to be rejected by this group."

"Who am I to share information with a group?"

"Nobody is going to be interested in what I have to say."

"People will be judging and criticizing me."

"People will see my flaws and shortcomings."

"I am a fraud."

On the other hand, a person who experiences joy, excitement, and expansion when engaging with public speaking is likely to be aligning with belief systems such as these.

"I get to share my gifts and talents with others."

"I have an opportunity to support and touch the lives of others."

"I have nothing to prove and nothing to hide. I can trust that others will either resonate or not resonate with who I am."

"My confidence and self-esteem are not derived from whether a group of people likes or dislikes my message."

"Life is about growth and evolution. It's about stepping into the unknown and being willing to engage with what shows up in the moment.

"I am an imperfect progressionist who is excited about the journey at hand."

"I can only fail if I give up on myself. Otherwise, I get to either learn or celebrate success."

During the six months of my baptism of fire, I got to explore a variety of belief systems that created a negative fear-based experience.

One of the core learnings that I realized was, I believed I was separate from universal intelligence. I thought I needed to take enormous action so that I could become someone that people respected as successful.

Through the process of reflection and then accessing the unconscious mind, I decided to let go of this belief paradigm, and I started the journey of coming home to my true nature.

The second significant realization I experienced was when I gained an understanding of the nature of reality. I am a soul. The word SOUL stands for Singular Outlet of Universal Love. I like to imagine it as a single ray of light beaming off the sun. This ray of light is whole, perfect, and complete. It is always radiating its nature and purpose out into the cosmos. The divine spark within me lies dormant unless I choose to activate and align it with the I AM presence within.

The soul has a higher mind, which is an aspect of self which is standing on top of a mountain. It can look down at all the infinite pathways and choices that exist as potentials in life. I realized that, if I can consciously tap into my intuition, which runs through my imagination, then I can receive insights and hunches that transcend what my rational mind currently believes to be true. For the first time, I found a way that supported me to expand my current reality, to access ideas and possibilities that existed in the space of "I don't know what I don't know."

The brain is like a quantum computer. It can shift into a multitude of different brain wave states. Each brain wave state allows me to access a different reality subset. For example, high beta is considered the normal waking state, which is the usual busyness occupied by people during the day. The alpha state is the space for creativity and imagination. All the great inventors, artists, musicians, scientists, and performers access this state to receive new information and ideas that are often revolutionary to what was previously known. The theta state is the space to access the subconscious and unconscious mind. The subconscious executes the creation of reality, where the unconscious is where all the automatic behavioral patterns are stored. All belief systems exist within the unconscious and run on autopilot. To change a belief system, you must first access the theta frequency domain. Delta is a very deep sleep state. Gamma is the channeling state where you receive instant downloads and communicate with other beings in other dimensions or realities.

It was January 2013 and I had emerged from the baptism of fire. After the collapse of the Shine core team, I was sitting in a room with three other inspirational visionary coaches. I had joined the Shine core team in October 2012 to assist in creating online education programs and be a part of a thriving global community. Shine focused on delivering events based around connection, purpose, and money. Unfortunately, that Shine team dissolved and, yet again, one door closed, which invited the opening of a new door. Love Intelligence was born, a company whose mission was to bring heart-based values leadership into the corporate world.

For the next nine months, the team worked tirelessly in creating the brand blueprint, crafting various offerings and forging alliances with an organization called Humanity in Business. Humanity in Business created live events to help corporate-minded business people to shift their perspectives from profit-only results to those that included win/win situations for business, humanity, and the planet. This was about riding the wave of change from organizations such as Plan B and Mindvalley, forging a new legacy in the business world, challenging the status quo.

Love Intelligence had agreed to have its branding professionally done through a contract deal worth twenty-five thousand dollars. The agreement was for Love Intelligence to go through a comprehensive branding and communication process in exchange for everyone in the marketing company to go through our newly crafted training programs. The CEO of the marketing company had gone through an awakening and knew the value of supporting his people to find their power, creativity, and leadership.

In October 2013, Suzie, one of our co-founders, and I were up in Byron Bay on behalf of Love Intelligence presenting at the Humanity's Event, which was a spin-off from the Neil Donald Walsh movement, Conversations with God. We had successfully delivered a segment to a welcoming and warm audience. Afterwards, we were celebrating our successes in a restaurant when I started to feel some strange, unsettling intuitive feelings. I said to Suzie, "It feels like some big changes are about to happen, but I am not sure what this means." Lo and behold, a few days later at the Love Intelligence team meeting back in Sydney, two of the four partners felt they were no longer in alignment with the company and wanted to leave immediately.

This was heartbreaking, as we had all put in so much energy and love into our program's creation. We were on the brink of signing new contracts and were gaining momentum for training deliveries.

A month later, in heartbreak, I found myself at my very first vipassana, a ten-day silent meditation retreat. I knew that I needed to go within myself to gain clarity on my next steps in life. I felt a sense of confusion and doubt fogging my mind. Maybe following the path of coaching and helping others wasn't for me. I felt a sense of surrendering in my heart. I realized that what I wanted was just to follow my soul's calling. What was it that I was meant to be doing on the earth at this time?

In the first seven days in the vipassana silent retreat. I was noticing pulsing tension in my right hip. The guides of the retreat told us that all the negative energies would begin to purge through the body in the form of feeling aches and pains. I was shocked by how strongly the mind and the body were interconnected. The powerlessness that had been running the show during 2013 began surfacing. By bringing my awareness and breath to these uncomfortable feelings, I was able to release and let the waves of energy go.

At the end of this silent retreat, I held a strong intention of knowing my next step in life. The answer gently came through, which was, "It is time to believe in yourself! It is time to reclaim your power. It is time to create your own unique vision and not piggyback off the potentially successful vision of others."

Again, I had been invited to come back home within myself—not to look for the answers outside of myself—to allow what is not in truth to be burnt up and dissolved. The lesson of surrendering and letting go was genuinely epic at this time in my life.

What none of the partners had realized in Love Intelligence or Shine was that the seeds we had all sown together had resulted in giving our individual power away to another person in the team—as we all believed that, because of this one person, success was imminent. The hard lesson that each of us had to take away was the need to reclaim our individual power and self-belief, knowing that we all are enough to create our heart's desires and highest callings.

Upon returning from the retreat, many new doors started to open. I was led to create a new soulful brand blueprint, which was the birthing of Lionheart Coaching. I received marketing, website, and social media support. I attracted three new clients relatively quickly.

With very little money in my bank account, I was given a choice to navigate the unknown by one of two ways.

1) Seeing life as a curious and exciting adventure. Believing that I am supported and that life has my back.

For me to be able to hold this perspective as true, I had to go deep within myself and ask, "Who and what am I?" I kept getting an energetic resonance that I am a son of the One infinite creator. I am made in the image of the ONE. Therefore, my existence is proof that I am already one hundred percent worthy, valuable, supported, deserving, capable, loved, and abundant. My role in the human game was to attune myself like a radio back to the frequencies of this bandwidth.

The other option was:

2) Seeing life as doom and gloom. Believing that I have to make it happen, that it will require enormous action and force to push my way out into the world to make my life work. This would result in a constant battle, heaviness, and burden. This means perceiving my life as separate from everything and everyone and aligning to a mentality of lack and limitation. This reality would kill a person's dreams and cause him/her to

fall back into getting a predictable, safe job and to sacrifice his soul's calling for comfort, security, belonging, validation, and approval.

About two weeks after holding the frequency aligned with the first choice, I received a miracle that boosted my spirits enormously. I unexpectedly received a twenty-thousand-dollar interest-free loan for eighteen months from the bank. This would be more than enough to allow me to launch and elevate my business from the ground up.

I applied to attend the Awesomeness Fest in Phuket which would be taking place in June 2014, and I was accepted. I felt that doors were opening where only walls had been before.

The next massive initiation for me was the putting together of the corporate training programs that our former company, Love Intelligence, had promised to deliver as part of the contra deal. We had a choice to walk away. Two of us chose to fulfill the agreement despite the branding for Love Intelligence going to waste.

The creative tension was palpable for me. A fear of mine that surfaced was being seen in large groups of people. What amplified this fear was the presence of alpha male energy within a group. Just imagine a pack of wolves sitting around a fire, listening to every word you are saying, waiting for you to slip up to have the excuse of tearing you to pieces. I knew that I needed a miracle to have the confidence and courage to face a large group of fifty dynamic, mostly alpha men, to guide them through the journey successfully.

Two months earlier, I had gone to a full moon sound ceremony. It was a crystal-clear night with the full moon radiating its mesmerizing essence to the earth. Upon the completion of the event, I looked up to the moon and asked in my heart, "What would it take for me to be able to effortlessly handle and enjoy this corporate delivery?"

My answer arrived sooner rather than later.

I arrived home that night and got into a fiery conversation with my flatmate. He asked how my work was evolving, and I shared with excitement. To my dismay, he began criticizing and tearing apart the successes and universal synchronicities I was experiencing.

I felt this intense fire energy bubble up in my belly. It began expanding and expanding. Something within me burst forth. I stood up and assertively told him, "That is not okay!" He ran to his bedroom and the fire that I had been lacking was now truly ignited.

This fire stayed in my belly for the next four months. When I entered the corporate boardroom to deliver the rollout of the training program, I felt a level of confidence and strength that I had never experienced before in my life. It felt like someone else was speaking through me. The right words in the proper order were just effortlessly flowing out. My voice was clear and strong and packed a punch. Everyone was paying attention. Everyone was listening.

We successfully delivered the corporate trainings and much transformation and change unfolded for the individuals in the company. Again, I was reminded to come back within myself and to say yes to the unknown. The creative tension of running those corporate training programs provided a pathway of change and transformation. I had to make a decision in my heart by saying yes and trusting the unfolding process.

Over an intensive growth phase from the collapse of Love Intelligence to the successful delivery of a values-based leadership training, I learned that the worldview I held to be true would determine what was unfolding in my life. By perceiving the world as not having enough, or believing that I am not enough, or believing that I am not capable or powerful enough to create the life of my dreams, I am allowing those beliefs to solidify and reinforce themselves over and over again. It becomes a self-fulfilling prophecy.

The edge of my comfort zone is like touching an electric fence. The beliefs that I currently hold to be true within my worldview will electrocute me away from the edge of my comfort zone. The inner saboteur will rear its head to push me back into safety, comfort, and predictability. Growth and expansion are not found in the comfort zone. I have to take a leap of faith into the unknown and trust that I will learn the lessons needed to take the next step in my life.

Each time I was required to step into a new space, the common factor that urged me to move forward was coming back into my heart. I began to feel an omnipresent beingness, observing and experiencing everything without judgment. It forced me to get out of the monkey mind and sink into a space of possibility and deep inner knowing. I had to allow life to flow and get out of my own way, and I did so when I began to focus on trusting that life is working out for me, even if I cannot always see the unfolding path.

Failure only happens when you give up on your dreams and yourself. Making a mistake is only taking a step forward in life and having your foot to land in an unexpected place. Either you receive a lesson to support the cultivation of experience and wisdom, or you get to celebrate for stepping beyond your current comfort zone. Both are wins! It is more useful to see life as an unfolding journey with you progressing and evolving over time. Letting go of the need to get everything right or perfect will significantly help you to break free from the judgments and limitations that hold so many people back from their wildest dreams.

Whenever you consider creating anything that goes beyond your current reality experience, naturally, you will get in touch with the underlying fears and limiting beliefs that have held you back. The process of creating and visioning goes hand in hand with transformation. Investing in yourself by learning how to confidently navigate life with effective tools, techniques, and perspectives to engage in life is essential. Accessing that inner strength and conviction will support the momentum of moving forward in your journey. Such an investment is wise and will reap dividends in the years ahead.

I am most grateful for the many mentors and teachers who have touched my life. Without receiving their guidance, I would not be where I am now. I encourage you to consider working with a mentor or guide to move into a realm of self-empowerment and creatorship. The vast majority of humanity is operating within survival and victim consciousness, which is laced with the experience of stress, anxiety, and worry. Learn the metaphysical rules of being and place both hands on the wheel of your life so that you navigate your own way.

Do you wait for a crisis or for a Mack truck to run you over before you awaken violently out of the autopilot dream? Alternatively, come back into your heart to a place beyond making sense, in innocence, and allow the next step to be revealed to you. Your true nature already knows the best path forward. Fear dissolves in the face of your all-connected real life because the illusion of separation rapidly melts away. What new choice is bubbling deep within your heart right now?

I invite you to explore the lessons and opportunities that your fears have been teaching you over the course of your life. Having an honest and open-hearted exploration of the choices you have made will shake and break the automatic, unconscious narrative that has been leading you.

As I reflect on the enormous changes that took place within my life, I find that the very experiences I wanted to avoid like the plague turned out to be the most powerful alchemical moments in my life. I had been living a life of certainty, predictability, and safety, and this all got turned upside down after leaving the corporate world and then supporting Ralph in his vision and work. Each step I took often invited me to come back into the abyss of the unknown—to let go of control and the sense that I knew where I was going. The magic and the miracles of life unfold in the unknown, and the only place of certainty that you will find is within your own being.

Isn't it time to come home to yourself? I know that this choice, despite being scary, was the greatest choice I have made in my life.

"The moment that you turn and face your fears is the moment that your fears turn to dust."

~ Kerryn Slater

CHAPTER TEN

---◆---

Faith Over Fear

Jayma Lyn G. Day

**"Living with fear stops us taking risks,
and if you don't go out on the branch,
you're never going to get the best fruit."**

~ Sarah Parish

As humans, I believe that we all have different fears; it is just in our nature.
We all have significant events in our lives, and none of us can escape from our first major life event, which is when we were born—that innocent period of life when we are not afraid of anything and don't know how to worry. We just cry when we feel uncomfortable or hungry. As the days pass by, we learn to fear something, and we are looking for someone we can trust who makes us feel secure and safe. This continues until we gradually and repeatedly face our fearful situations and get over them.

Before I say more, I must say that it's an honor to share my experience with readers from around the world. I appreciate the opportunity to share how I deal with my fears and what has made me a better person. I hope that you can relate to my story and that it might give you the courage to overcome your own fears.

I grew up on a farm, typically located in the scenic countryside of San Juan Delfin Albano, Isabela, Philippines. I learned as I saw my parents and family work long, hard hours within flexible schedules. It was fun to play and just get dirty, feeding the animals and working outdoors.

I was nine years old when my sister graduated from high school. It was 1990, and my parents decided to go abroad and work in Portugal. They gave up the farmer's life because they were afraid it wasn't generating enough income for my sister's and my education fees. My mother was a cook at The U.S. Diplomat's house in Lisbon, and my father was a gardener at the U.S. Embassy, Lisbon.

My family also feared that we might lose everything because my father was involved with the wrong people who led him into gambling and drinking alcohol. I was afraid and hid under the table every time he was drunk. I was worried that he might hurt my mother, as he had done many times in the past.

My mother was a victim of domestic violence. She tried to leave my father many times, but they always reconciled and got back together. My mother did not want to have a broken family. She chose to sacrifice her own happiness to keep our family together. But every time my father would get drunk, we all feared that he might hurt my mother again.

My father lost a lot of money and land. That's one of the reasons my parents needed to leave the Philippines, to try to prevent us from losing everything. When they made more money in Portugal, they bought back the piece of land that my father had sold. They invested in a rice farm, but he still spent more money on alcohol and drinking with his friends. I thought he would change, and I truly hoped he would change, but I didn't know when it might happen or what God's plan might be. He retired from the U.S. Embassy and received compensation for his 15 years of service. Unfortunately, he spent most of that money on alcohol and refused to admit that he had a problem.

When my parents and older sister moved to Portugal, I stayed with my grandparents in the Philippines. Those were times of fear and sadness and longing for love and care and inspiration. Longing for someone to appreciate my achievements and sacrifices, I did my best to finish my studies even though I was miles away from my loved ones. All I had was my faith, and I believed God was ever present.

For a long time, I was afraid of being alone. I knew I would miss my family. No one would be there to help me with my homework and school projects. Every time I missed my parents and my sister, my pillow became my buddy at night.

After I graduated from high school, I studied at La Consolacion College, Manila. I studied hotel and restaurant management. I was afraid to fail; I did not want to waste my parents' hard-earned money after they had sacrificed for us to have an education. My sister and I did our best to not waste money, and we intended to repay our parents for all of their hard work and sacrifices.

One of the many life lessons that I learned in college was through all the many twists and turns that life offers. I learned that we must face our fears. This act of courage makes life more comfortable in the long run. If you don't meet your fear, your fear will control you instead of you controlling it. I know that some things in life are tough to face, but if you believe in yourself and do what you think is right, your fears will slowly slip away. There's nothing more powerful than your faith when you believe you are capable of overcoming any obstacle in your way.

After I graduated from college in August 2000, my parents invited me to Portugal. I found work and started building my life and working to make my dreams come true. My first job was as a receptionist for Hotel Veneza in Lisbon. I wanted to get a residence permit in Portugal. I applied to the Australian Embassy Residence to work at the Australian Ambassador's official home and left my job at the hotel. I applied what I had studied and learned in cooking, table setting, and serving when they had receptions, hosting dinners, meetings, and lunches.

I lived in the greater area of Lisbon, and in the beginning, I found difficulty in adapting to life there. I experienced culture shock, as I didn't speak the language. I also missed my sister in the Philippines, although Portugal is one of the safest and most affordable countries in Europe and the people there are friendly. My dream was to make the embassy successful and to support and provide a good future for my children. I applied all my experiences in life at the embassy. It was my outlet when I was feeling down, raising my mood through cooking. I learned every job for different events and for different people, and I built relationships with customers.

But there are always situations that we can't control. I met a guy who stole my heart. I trusted that he would love me. He was a seaman and worked on a ship. When the ship docked in Portugal for three months, we were introduced by my parents' friend. This man promised my parents that he would take care of me. My parents' expectations of me were high, so when I learned that I was pregnant out of wedlock, they didn't want me to marry him because he already had a wife and children in the Philippines. When the relationship ended, I tried to get back on my feet and pick up the broken pieces.

After I gave birth to Jairo on September 11, 2006, it was hard for me to find work. When he was seven months old, I sent him to the Philippines. I hired a full-time baby sitter and my sister supervised everything for me. I went to the United States to work, but loneliness was slowly destroying me and I hated being away from my son. I saved as much money as I could by working two jobs as a caregiver during the week and a babysitter during the weekends. After nine months, I saved enough money to take Jairo back to Portugal with me.

When I met Jairo's father, I thought it was real love, but then it was another experience of fear. I even asked myself what did I do to deserve this? I didn't deserve his treatment, but how about my son? Even though I handled the responsibility as a single mother with the help of my family, and we provided for Jairo's needs, it was a very difficult time for me. But there were lessons to learn from it.

Only after I'd had that dark experience of Jairo's father leaving me did I find a way to connect with myself and ask my myself many questions about what I was going to do. What was I passionate about? I started attending workshops to discover my calling. It took some time for me to gain trust, to heal myself, and to recover. This is how I discovered my joy of cooking.

Then the opportunity finally came for me to make my dream come true and own my first restaurant serving diplomats in Lisbon. I was excited to meet new people who became my daily customers, and my son would entertain them by talking about football while they drank coffee. It was a great experience, but unfortunately, it didn't last long. My father came to the restaurant drunk and demanded I serve him wine. I refused, as he was already drunk. That's when he started breaking things. I was afraid! My father wanted to hit me with a chair. I was scared that he would hurt my son, so I just protected him and hugged him tight while he was screaming Mama! He was afraid, too, that I might get hurt. Finally, someone called the police to stop him from breaking things. He calmed down and went home. My staff were terrified, and I was stressed and shaking. What if something had happened to me? Who would take care of my son?

I met my husband, Michael, in 2011. He became my best friend, my mentor, and then my husband. He is the one who recharged me when I'm tired from running the restaurant. After the incident at the restaurant with my father, my husband recommended that we close the doors. Michael told me that it was not the right time for this business and that I first needed to take care of Jairo. I listened to him, and I learned from the experience.

I love my parents, but I was so young when they left that it has been hard to bridge the gap. To this day, I still long for their love and care. My father's mentality is different. He thinks that paying for my sister's and my educations is enough and is an expression of his love for us.

But in 2013, I saved his life. I came home and saw him lying on the floor. He'd had a big stroke. I called the ambulance and took him to the hospital. My mother was in Italy at that time and my sister was in the Philippines. Whatever my father's indiscretions towards us were, he is still our father, and we give respect and try to forgive him. The hospital where he was admitted was close to my work in Lisbon. I went there during my lunch break and fed him. He spent 15 days in the ICU. We thought he would not make it, but it was a miracle. I don't know how. Even the doctors were amazed. After a few months of recovery, he went back to alcohol and was diagnosed with dementia. It was terrible and a source of stress because my husband was diagnosed with lung cancer at the same time.

Michael and I supported each other emotionally through many ups and downs in life. In July 2015, we ran to the emergency because Michael was having difficulty breathing. We found from his x-ray that he had something in his lungs. The doctor recommended that we see a specialist. This was another fear that had an impact on our life. We found out that he had a tumor on the lower lobe of his left lung. He'd never smoked, and he is health-conscious, exercising every day. He has an athletic build and is fit. So why him?

As we faced this life-threatening situation, we did our best to take care of the things that we could control. We don't know why he got sick. Before our wedding anniversary, he had the operation and removed the lower lobe of his lung. We were afraid, but all we could do was pray.

It was stressful for me because, during Michael's recovery, the aftermath of my father's stroke lead him into dementia; this with his alcoholism made for a bad combination. There was a lot of fear and frustration for everyone around him when he drank. Sometimes we had to call the police again, but they couldn't do anything. We had many sleepless nights, and the next day I would go to work without rest.

"Being brave isn't the absence of fear. Being brave is having that fear but finding a way through it."

~ Bear Grylls

All I can do is live day by day, facing my fears and overcoming them one at a time. Dreams aren't meant to die, and life must go on.

In February 2017, I was accepted for a training program called HIVE in San Francisco, California. It was a great experience with 143 participants from many different countries. It was intensive training and I dug into my passion and purpose in business to pursue what I love. I've transformed my business into events and catering. While working at the Australian Embassy Residence as a cook, I worked with some events and catered to the Philippine Embassy as well. Then I was recommended to other ambassadors and other diplomats. I decided to open actively and named my events catering service after my restaurant, A Diplomata. Most of my customers are diplomats, so I thought I would keep the name.

It has been a good experience; every event is different, and I manage to cater for up to 300 people at a time. I am happy to feed the Philippine Embassy with their honorable guests, such as artists, senators, and diplomats. I am so glad that my work has been recognized. Since I began my business, I have also opened a store in Belem in the Lisbon area where I sell international food ingredients. Now I am the founder of A Diplomata, a mother of two beautiful boys, Jairo and William Michael, a wife, a chef, and a daughter.

Through all of my experiences while dealing with my fears, I have learned to create an action plan. Here is my advice to get through the scary times.

1. Know That Fear Is Real, but It Can Be Overcome.

    - Right now, around the world, people are facing fear — real fear. This is the kind of fear that I pray my children and I will never experience.

When I look at the world we all live in. I find that fear, like so many other emotions, can mean so many different things to so many different people, such as

- A child who has to be physically dragged to school on the first day
- The walk down a dark corridor late at night alone
- The woman who is told, "We are sorry; we can't help you."
- When you find out the person you trusted fooled you
- The first time you become pregnant and are facing a responsibility created by someone you trusted
- Facing the judge to get full custody of one's child
- Having a car accident with your small child in the vehicle
- Witnessing a parent facing death from a stroke
- Having a spouse diagnosed with cancer
- Facing bankruptcy and possibly losing a business.

These fears have had a different impact on my life than they might have on another person's life, and I find that facing them has helped me to be the stronger person that I am today.

2. Accept Your Fear.

- We are quick to say, "I can't moan; my life is not as bad as X." While, in theory, that's honorable, your appreciation of Mr. or Mrs. X's horrific life won't change anything directly. So, accept that your fear is relevant to you.

3. Get Some Perspective.

We know something is scary, and yet we still do it. Why? Because we have a perspective on fear. When you lose perspective, it can feel too big and too scary.

Look around you to get some perspective on your fear.

- Are you really at risk?
- Will this kill you?
- If the worst were to happen, what would that look like?

4. Hold a Hand.

For the child petrified of the thunderstorm or the teen who can't get back in a car again after failing her driving test, your job as a parent is to reassure, encourage, enable, and motivate them to courageously face something they never would choose to do again.

We know many of our fears aren't real. However, only when someone guides us with love, respect, and safety—and without judgment—are we able to get through anxiety. And trust me, you can get through your fears. I've seen it so many times.

Ask yourself

- If the worst were to happen, what would that be?
- Could that happen?
- If the worst did happen, how would you recover?
- If the worst were to happen, what would you need to do next?

By seeing fear as not the end destination but part of being human, you can see through its wily evil ways and move forward.

5. Know Whose Hand You Hold, Either Physically or Emotionally.

This helps with fears for the rest of your life. You can get as many friends as you want, but not all of them understand your concerns, emotions, and feelings. And just a few are truly willing to hold your hand when you need it the most. Surround yourself with your loved ones and with people who you can learn from.

It is with profound gratitude that I acknowledge the people who have supported me in my life's journey.

Can you overcome all of your fears?

Of course, you can! It's possible! All you do is start and take one step at a time. If you don't quit, you'll soon have a few hundred steps behind you. You will make it, and you will never forget it!

We can go through tough times with surviving powers!

This divine quality of dreaming what you want to be, where you want to go, and what you'd love to do fills you with hope to achieve the goals you have set for yourself. All of this makes you human—a unique creature in all of creation!

Faith is a choice. It is a decision. It is a commitment. It can be defined as wanting more out of life. Faith helps you develop courage needed to overcome any fear in your life.

It's been an honor to share my experience with readers from around the world. I appreciate the opportunity to share how I deal with my fears and what has made me a better person. I hope that you can relate to my story and that it might give you the courage to overcome your own fears.

"Life is found in the dance between your deepest desire and your greatest fear."

~ Anthony Robbins

CHAPTER ELEVEN

————◆◆◆————

Dancing with Fears

By Peggy Liling Chen

**"I am the master of my fate,
I am the captain of my soul."**

Invictus, by William Ernest Henley

The very first time I thought about suicide, I was ten. Shocked? Me too.

I wrongly believed the negative message from my childhood which told me that I didn't deserve anything good, love included, because I was "merely" a girl. I even thought that I shouldn't have been born at all because of my gender.

I was born into a very traditional Taiwanese family. This meant there was a strong requirement for sons, not the five daughters my parents had. Strict expectations and pressure were put on my mother by my grandmother. It was torture for all of us. From my blurry memory, I don't recall directly feeling any love and affection from my grandmother, although it's unfair to say since she can't explain herself here. Even so, three decades later, I finally reconciled with my grandmother, spiritually, through the teacher training program of the Heal Your Life Workshop created by Louise Hay.

Most of the time in my childhood, I barely experienced love, affection, respect, or trust from my family or witnessed affection between my parents, as their parents had arranged their marriage. My parents' marriage was more like a job, with the main aim of having a son to carry on the family name. My mother did not only marry one man, but also a whole family. She was not allowed to have a voice or stand up for herself, and certainly not for her daughters, because girls were useless and worthless. This wasn't strange for most people back in that time. Indeed, it was typical of most families, especially in rural Taiwan.

I very rarely saw my mother being happy, especially when my grandparents paid a visit, normally staying with us for a few weeks, sometimes longer. My mother would be like a rabbit in a little cage. She was worried about her or us making any mistakes or doing anything to annoy my grandparents. I could sense her fears, which always made me feel sad for her and angry with myself, my grandparents, and my father. I blamed myself for causing her trouble by being born the wrong gender; I blamed my grandparents for daring to treat my mother so harshly; I blamed my father for being irresponsible and uncaring towards his wife.

At the same time, I planted a seed of thought in my mind that men were unreliable and uncaring towards their spouses. I took my mother's fear, and, later in my life, I often attracted men who were unreliable or irresponsible or uncaring towards me.

It was hard to see my mother living in fear most of the time. She didn't enjoy her life at all. I never heard any word of compliment or appreciation for my mother from my grandparents or my father. Instead, my grandparents—especially my grandmother—were generally demanding and complained that my mother was unqualified to be a good wife because she couldn't have a baby boy. My father always kept silent. I suppose he chose flight when he had fears, mainly because he didn't want to deal with the conflict between his mother and his wife.

At the age of ten, being the oldest daughter, I was expected to assist my mother in caring for my younger sisters. I became a little mother, and I lost my freedom just as my mum had. It was a clear message that impacted my life, and I made up my mind to not have children of my own.

My mum was resented by my father, who actually didn't know how to get along with the wife he didn't really know. Even worse, he became obsessed with gambling over the years, causing intense mistrust in their marriage. My mum was also resented by my grandmother, who kept blaming her for being unable to have a son and ignored how hardworking she was. My mother even seemed to resent herself for not daring to stand up for herself, and she also carried resentment towards all of her daughters who, at ten, eight, five, and four, cried a lot and were not independent enough.

She hid her resentment from my grandparents but expressed her anger in front of us. Sometimes, she would lose her temper. It was terrifying to hear my mum yelling at us: "I wish I'd never given birth to you!" I was too young to understand all the pain of my parents and grandparents. I only knew that none of them were happy most of the time. I drew my own conclusion: because I was not a boy, I was naturally not good enough and that caused them to have unhappy lives.

I always had a thought in my mind: *What if I had been a boy? My parents and grandparents would have been happier. My mother's life would have been easier.* It was all my fault. I was a mistake. But I didn't know how to deal with the fears. It felt so confusing, pathetic, and strange. It seemed like I was watching my family perform a terrible dance that they'd never learned properly, letting their fears lead. They stepped on each other's feet in panic, they pushed each other rudely, they resentfully blamed each other, always expressing the same message: "I am right; you are wrong! Poor me. They all hate me, and we all hate you!" I was deeply frustrated by the misleading message I learned from them.

I didn't even acknowledge that the fears were within me. There was no one I could share my feelings and emotions with. All I could do was push them all down into my inner self. The fears were named *You are not good enough, You are a mistake, You are worthless and useless,* and *It's all your fault that your mother is disrespected and lives unhappily.*

One day, an idea suddenly ran through my mind: *It would be better if you die; that would benefit everyone.* It sounded odd, but I tried to make it happen. Thank God, I was too young to let the fears drive me completely. Subconsciously or knowingly—I'm not sure which—I just wanted to have some attention and care from my parents, but I had never learned how to ask for it because it felt like I wasn't allowed to. I tied a ribbon tightly around my neck on several occasions, tighter and tighter each time. I can still vividly remember the feeling the last time I tried. It felt like the blood was all gone from my brain; everything turned to darkness and the pressure on my throat took my breath.

I heard two voices in my mind. One said, "Hey, you've almost made it. You've done an excellent job. Keep trying!" The other said, "Your parents would be distraught. It's not right." I didn't know which voice I should listen to. Just before I lost consciousness, some other school kids saw what was happening, screamed, ran to find a teacher, and I stopped. Later that day when I went home from school, the teacher phoned my parents and told them what had happened. They asked me why I had done it. I pretended that it wasn't a big deal and told them I was just curious and wanted to be cool. They said, "Don't do it again; you could die."

They didn't show or express too much emotion, or perhaps that was how they expressed emotion and concern. I didn't tell them how much I worried and feared that they didn't love or care about me. Regardless, I thought that, at least, they had taken some time, paid attention, and asked me what had happened; that gave me some comfort. The fear of dying saved me from the fear of not being loved.

I survived, but I hadn't yet learned how to face and deal with my concerns, and those concerns grew up with me. As a little child, I always sought approval from my parents and grandparents. And so I wanted to join their family dance even though it was a total mess.

It was not easy for my parents to raise five children in a working class family. My father was a blue-collar worker with low pay. Besides, when he was younger, he sometimes hid money for gambling, which really upset my mother a lot. I remember one night when I was eight or nine. I was at home alone because my mother was helping my grandmother take care of my ill grandfather. I was waiting for my father to come home.

When the sky turned dark, all those scary stories started playing in my head. I was more and more scared. At around 8 p.m., my mother called and discovered that my father had not come home yet, and she became very angry. She asked me to check if some money she had hidden was still in the pocket of a jacket in the closet in their bedroom. I looked and told her there was no money at all. She was furious. She immediately expressed her anger and blamed my father for being irresponsible and untrustworthy and kept saying how poor we were.

I was terrified. Again, I felt it was all my fault. I felt so sad, helpless, and angry at myself because I couldn't help but feel anger towards my father. Inside, I felt abandoned. I didn't see my father that night. My mother asked one of my aunts to take me to her home and keep me with them for a few days. That night I learned the new fears of being abandoned and of being very poor. For people who were from poor families, opportunities were as limited as money.

This was not an entirely bad experience. From it I learned that I really wanted to earn money and be independent as soon as possible. It felt so bitter, painful, and lacking in freedom to stay at home with its atmosphere of disappointment. Carrying all of those fears made me feel like people disapproved of me. The more I thought I was not appreciated, the more I wanted to prove to people that they were wrong. I acted like a warrior preparing to fight and defend myself at any time.

I tried so hard to fight for my destiny because I thought I had to. I lived in the mode of fight-or-flight most of the time because of all my fears burning inside me. I spent most of my energy denying my worries instead of openly facing them. My fears were like unfriendly dance partners assigned by the instructor. Their name was Uncertainty. I hated this arrangement, but I couldn't escape it. Begrudging these enforced partners, I thought, "Okay, fine! I will fight back and be the worst dance partner possible until I drive you away!"

I chose to fight the resentment and disapproval. The fight against my fears somehow helped me develop the courage to make important decisions and to take action to accomplish them, even though some of these decisions were not what my mother expected from me. It was hilarious that, although my mother was so unhappy with her marriage and life, she thought I should have the same experience as she had. She thought that was a woman's fate. Seeing her life, I felt the opposite. The only thing I desired was getting out of that life and leaving that home as soon as possible. I never wanted to copy my mother's life at all. I just wanted to run away. The fear of becoming my mother helped me to become stronger and more independent and to pursue my own destiny.

Proving myself became the defining motivation of my life because of the fear of not being good enough. And therefore, a battling journey unfolded. However, under my warrior-like face of toughness and feigned masculinity, the inner little girl was terrified and helpless.

No matter what, the fears kicked my ass. I had a fear of being poor, so I proved that I could earn money and got my first wages when I was ten years old. I feared that being a girl was worthless and I wasn't supposed to aspire to have a higher education, so I tried my best and passed the university entrance exam, making me the first person in my whole extended family to go to university.

After spending years learning and practicing hard, there were several times when I wrested the lead in our dance from my fears. However, most of the time I had no control at all. I had a fear that I didn't deserve good things and I had to work very hard to earn money, which caused me to lose all the money I had made and get in a big debt crisis, having to take two full-time jobs and work like a dog for six years to get myself out of it. I feared that I was not valuable; it was very shameful and painful when I was dismissed from my job. After all, I'd really enjoyed that job and had always worked hard. I thought I was pretty good, but it turned out I was not valued.

I tried my best to prove that I was fearless. However, it didn't work. I fought everything in my life because I was worried that I would lose. The more I fought against my fears, the more power those fears gained; it didn't matter if I proved I was right. A long while later, I learned the simple explanation is that energy attracts like energy. As it turned out, I was giving most of my energy and attention to fears instead of love; I paid the most attention to proving myself externally instead of trying to be at peace with myself.

Before dancing with any partners or fears harmoniously and beautifully, the most important thing is to learn the essential dance steps—self-acceptance and self-love—which I only acknowledged and learned several years later.

My energy was running out after fighting with my fears for such a long time. I lost my strength. Through all those years, I earned money and lost money and got in debt; I was in love with a wonderful man, but he was not available; I had a great job, and I was laid-off. I thought everything was under control, but, ironically, everything was out of control.

I was so frustrated and scared by this pattern—having it and losing it—that I allowed it to drive me to behave differently when I moved to China and started a new job. I was so afraid of losing my job again that I could not be myself. I started trying so hard to please my VIP colleagues, brown-nosing my boss and other people in higher positions, that it made me lose my sense of self. At the same time, I blamed and impatiently yelled at the staff under me. When I finished work, I just felt so angry and guilty. I didn't know what had happened to me. I was so scared of the uncertainty and couldn't see where my life was going.

The resentment, anger, hatred, and disgust all came along. It seemed to me that there was no one who I could trust and share with. I felt extremely lonely and manipulated by my fears. I suppressed all my feelings and emotions because it was too risky to open my heart.

I believed there was no way for me to change my life, although, perhaps, my subconscious mind really didn't want any change, as it felt good to play the victim. I lived like a zombie and played games of office-politics from day to day. I was lost and my mind was empty. Fears took control of my life.

However, love is actually all around. There was a gentleman who walked into my life. It was like all other romantic, loving relationships. We fell in love. We conquered obstacles together.

One time, we had a big fight during a Skype call because of my stress about work, my insecurity about our long-distance relationship, my doubts about why he wanted to be with me, you name it. Subconsciously, I couldn't bear the pain arising from the fear that I would lose all of these wonderful and sweet things again because I didn't deserve them. It absolutely terrified me. I drank a lot, got drunk, and was like a crazy woman crying on the call, accusing him of not caring about me because he ignored my messages, missed a few calls, and demanded we break up.

After all of this mess, I fell asleep. He kept watching me sleeping via Skype. He was not offended at all. Instead, he showed understanding and compassion for my sadness and insecurity. He was concerned for my well-being and wanted to support me in person through these difficult times, and hence he at once booked a flight and asked his boss for one week of personal leave. The next day he was on a flight to Beijing from London. He called me before boarding and said that he would be there with me. This young man completely opened my heart. We made commitments, and we married in Taiwan.

It was like a fairy tale that would end up with the beautiful princess and the prince living happily ever after.

Unfortunately, I didn't believe I was beautiful, nor did I think I was valuable like a princess. He was not a prince, even though he was from England. My fears didn't want me to believe that I could have this beautiful story in my world. It had already been a big challenge for me to deal with my own fears. And now my fears and I had new dance partners—my husband and his fears. The funny thing was, I had run away from home and avoided watching and participating in the unpleasant family dance, but I didn't even realize I was about to recreate it.

We purely and deeply loved, accepted, and supported each other. After so many years of looking for a so-called soulmate, I believed he was the one. In front of him, I didn't need to pretend. I could freely be who I was. Even though he was nine years younger than me, this young gentleman had a big heart and sincerely cared about and took care of me.

Yet somehow, it all felt too good to be true, and that triggered my deepest fear—having it all and then losing it because I didn't deserve love. These doubts led me to more and more what-if fear-based questions after we got married.

My subconscious mind started seeking negative hints and thoughts. One thought I believed very strongly and firmly was that this lovely man would definitely leave me because I was much older, I was ugly, and I didn't deserve this attractive man and the love he gave me. There was always a voice from the fears saying, "How could a normal young man love you? It's crazy that you believed it. You'll get hurt because he'll leave you." I was so terrified by the thought and the feeling that having something outstanding and losing it would be even more bitter and painful than never having it. I would prefer to have nothing at all than to have it and lose it.

And therefore, I was constantly busy creating dramas and finding any kind of excuse to blame him and push him away. It was like my subconscious wanted him to leave me to prove my theory was true, and I could then play the role of a pitiful victim. It was not fair to him after all of his efforts and sacrifices.

We went from being a lovely couple to an ugly one. We argued most of the time. The gap of understanding between us became wider and wider. He couldn't understand why I didn't want to move back to Taiwan as I was so unhappy and upset living in China. I blamed him and said he didn't understand that I had no choice. He claimed I just wanted to stay in my comfort zone, which prompted another fight between us, and so on.

We were triggered by fears. My negativities and fears finally resonated with him. One day, out of the blue, he announced that he didn't love me anymore and planned to return to England soon, even though he said sadly that it was painful to feel this way. My first response was, "I knew this day would come. I just knew it. I knew that I didn't deserve love." The fears owned me completely. I couldn't move a step any more. I let the fears manipulate me whichever way they wanted in our dance. I was hurt.

He was upset but still left a week later. Perhaps the distance brought back a little spark, which led us to agree to try again. This time it was my turn to leave everything behind and move to another country for the sake of our marriage, even though I had my concerns. I was so grateful to my former employer who accepted my request for a six-month leave without pay, so I had a back-up plan for myself if my marriage still couldn't be fixed after this attempt.

My marriage failed despite spending six months and all my savings in England trying to rescue it.

I felt myself to be a failure. I was ashamed, depressed, desperate, lonely, and hopeless. I was so scared by the thought that there was no one to love me anymore. It was heartbreaking, extremely painful. Strangely, I couldn't cry. I guess I was too sad to cry.

The darkness of fear covered me tightly. I felt like I was being pushed down to the bottom of the water. I couldn't breathe. I was painfully thrown away, pushed and dragged around again and again by my fears as if it were a fun game. In the darkness, I heard the fears snicker at me. And suddenly, there was a voice from within saying, "I have to go. I can't live like this anymore." The natural pursuit of well-being as a human was calling and made me decide to give up on saving my marriage and go back to Taiwan. So, I left my husband in England, albeit with a broken heart.

However, instead of seeking the pity and company of family and friends, I went to Bali. It was my first visit to Bali. It was not really for any special spiritual reason. Simply, the Malaysia Airlines flight was cheapest because one of their planes had crashed a week before. I felt I wouldn't mind dying in an air crash, as my heart was already dead.

Fortuitously, during my time in Ubud, the spiritual healer Ketut Liyer was still alive and I visited him. He was popular, having been introduced to the world in *Eat Pray Love* by Elizabeth Gilbert. I remember that I desperately asked Ketut if I could have a relationship and marry again. He smiled at me and kept saying the same things. "You're thrilled. You're very successful. You're very healthy. You will have a new boyfriend." I replied, "But I don't want a new boyfriend. I want my husband." He simply kept smiling and repeating the same words again and again:

"You are very happy."

"You are very successful."
"You are very healthy."
"You will have a new boyfriend."

Magically, I bought it. For some reason, it warmed me, encouraged and empowered me. It felt like my fears and I actually had a slow dance with hugs. We were finally more at ease together. A while later, when I started practicing positive affirmations, I realized that this had been my first experience of an affirmation bath, an exercise taught in Louise Hay's Heal Your Life Workshop.

Afterward, I decided to try something new, and I traveled to Lombok where I got a new key to open the next door on my spiritual journey. I had no idea what SUP was when I signed up. On the beach the next day, my SUP instructor introduced it to me: Stand Up Paddle, or paddle boarding!

I was terrified when I found out I had to take that board onto the ocean. Even worse, I would have to stand up on the board and PADDLE! How on earth could it work? I couldn't swim; I would die! The fears set an alarm ringing. Suddenly a thought flashed through my mind: *You are so funny. I thought you didn't care about dying anymore, as you consider your heart already dead.* My mind challenged my fears.

The instructor started his coaching session, which didn't give me enough time to wait for the argument to play out in my head. Instead, both my mind and my fears needed to concentrate on their new task. This time, they had to cooperate for the sake of my survival. It turned out to be the very first time my fears and mind managed to dance well and consciously together. They learned how to support and dance with each other. Acceptance and trust were built between them, helping them to release control and cease manipulation.

I don't remember how many times I fell into the water and how much water I drank. I just couldn't stand up and balance. My legs shook, and I was bloody scared. The fears yelled inside me and dragged me down into the water from time to time. My mind was busy trying to find a proper reason to make sense of why I wanted to do this. Apart from these negative voices, there was a voice from my heart saying, "Take this challenge. It will change your perspective of fear and life."

I crawled back up onto the board, tried to stand up, and fell into the water again. The instructor smiled empoweringly and said to me, "You are too afraid. Don't fear; you are safe. You are safe in the ocean. First of all, it's the ocean; you'll float as long as you relax. The more you try to be in control, the more of a struggle you'll have. Relax and follow the flow. Secondly, you are in a life-jacket that will keep you floating. And lastly, you are safe with me. I won't let you die, and I'm certain I can protect you. All you need to do is clear your mind and relax, okay?"

His words were persuasive and both my fears and my mind agreed with them. Inspiring instruction, indeed!

And he gave me a motivating lesson after I could finally stand up but still couldn't propel the board by paddling and had fallen into the water several more times. He encouraged me to get back on the board. I felt more comfortable sitting on the board this time.

He said, "When you're standing up and paddling, don't watch your feet, don't look down, look ahead."

He pointed to the mountains in the far distance and said to me, "Look at the mountains. That's the destination and the goal you want to reach. Look ahead and move forward." It was not only the best instruction for SUP for beginners but also a wise life lesson. His words awoke me from my fears and taught me how to face them and start over.

"Don't look down. Look ahead and move forward."

I finally realized that all of those fears I couldn't acknowledge were actually very normal, just a part of the human evolutionary inheritance which is supposed to help me to survive. However, they were intensified by all of the limiting beliefs and negative messages that I was taught growing up and chose to absorb. I used to try so hard to deny and fight all of my fears—to be fearless—but that gave the fears more validation and credit. The fact is, if we weren't afraid, we wouldn't survive for long. If the 10-year-old me hadn't been sufficiently afraid of death, I might have died already. And again, if I hadn't been terrified of being stuck in the unhappiest darkness after the separation from my ex-husband, I wouldn't have started my new journey of self-discovery.

After these years of learning and practice, I've realized that my fears actually just want to protect me and help me to survive. I sincerely appreciate that. But if I wish to survive and live well, I have to learn better how to recognize my fears and work with them. It means that I need to learn how to accept and appreciate the existence of concerns and increase my courage to challenge them and ask them to be quiet when they are screaming at me. Remembering the conversations with the SUP instructor on Lombok always warmly reminds me: I'm safe; I just need to relax, look ahead and move forward.

I had carried emotions of regret, low self-esteem, self-hatred, and self-loathing for decades, and those emotions were revealed through my marriage. I presented myself as a positive and enthusiastic person in front of people but hated myself behind the scenes. Louise Hay empowered me to believe that I could change. I started learning from her 12 Ways to Love Yourself from her bestselling book, *You Can Heal Your Life*. One afternoon in December 2014, in a hotel room in Shanghai, I cried like a baby after my first time reading it. I started practicing all of the tools and techniques taught by Ms. Hay.

About six months after starting these practices, I felt myself gradually changing. I felt and believed that I had the right, strength, and empowerment to create the life I wanted, which made me feel happier and more courageous and hopeful. The program encouraged me to take more action to step out of my former lifestyle. I started becoming an adventurous world traveler and explorer. With each new experiment and adventure, my fears and I learned how to face the uncertainties better in unison.

The relationship between my fears and me had improved wonderfully and continued to get better and better. We learned how to get along together more peacefully and trusted each other more. We enjoyed our time debating and understanding. When my concerns and I have disagreements, we try to help each other decide whether it's a fact or just a thought. Facing fears still sometimes feels scary, but it can be interesting as well. My fears have become more adaptable, flexible, and more willing to give me permission to explore and discover myself more deeply.

Two years later, in February 2017, I quit my job and moved to London from China and started an online business. It felt really good. A funny thing happened to me a few months after I settled in London: my fears actually encouraged me to take an eight-month coach training program. I argued with my worries that my English was not good enough to do the course. My fears told me that, rather than worrying whether my English skills were strong enough to understand the course, I was actually using that worry as an excuse to stay where I was. They told me that I was satisfied with my current skills and not really trying to advance them for the sake of improving my future. This surprising voice from my fears helped me to grow and develop myself and focus on creating a business I love. Good job, dear fears! I appreciate you for foreseeing the future for me.

I eventually completed the training program, understanding it fairly well and learning a lot from it. Happily, I have become a life and business coach. I reckon the more victories I have trying new things, the more comfortable the fears are and the more willing they are to let me try more.

It sounds awesome, doesn't it?

And now, I have loving and supportive relationships with my parents and my sisters. I've moved to Bali, the place I dreamed of living. My new perspectives and thoughts have created a new life, shaped by my values and purposes. I have caring and supportive friends all around the world and lots of love, fun, and joy in my life.

I'm running a project called The Power of Women, which supports women who want to create the lives they desire but don't dare or know how as they struggle with the limiting beliefs learned form society. This project has been helping thousands of women change the way they think, as well as their perspectives of themselves and of life itself, so that they can start pursuing their dreams.

And I've been creating a new online plan—Learning for English Learning, which is aimed at helping and supporting non-native English speakers to get along with their fears about learning and using English so that they can create the lives and careers they dream of having. With an actionable methodology, combined with the tools and techniques of Louise Hay's philosophies and the concept of Heal Your Life Workshop, as well as NLP, my mission is absolutely to help more people, especially women, to create and live the lives they desire and deserve.

In *A Course in Miracles*, Helen Schucman writes, "Whenever light enters darkness, the darkness is abolished. What you believe is true for you." This wise quote is always helpful for me when facing my fears. I get along well with my worries. We've had lots of conversations and made lots of compromises. We've done our best to build a new relationship together. I still have fears, but I've grown and learned to get along with them, and, in the end, I dance with my fears to create the life I love, because I know I'm always leading the dance.

"Avoiding danger is no safer in the long run than outright exposure. The fearful are caught as often as the bold."

~ Helen Keller

AUTHOR BIOGRAPHIES

John Spender

CHAPTER ONE

John Spender is a 21-time International Best Selling co-author, who didn't learn how to read and write at a basic level until he was ten years old. He has since traveled the world, started many businesses leading him to create the best-selling book series A Journey Of Riches. He is an Award Winning International Speaker and Movie Maker.

John worked as an international NLP trainer and has coached thousands of people from various backgrounds through all sorts of challenges. From the borderline homeless to very wealthy individuals, he has helped many people to get in touch with their truth to create a life on their terms.

John's search for answers to living a fulfilling life has taken him to work with Native American Indians in the Hills of San Diego, the forests of Madagascar, swimming with humpback whales in Tonga, exploring the Okavango Delta of Botswana and the Great Wall of China. He's traveled from Chile to Slovakia, Hungary to the Solomon Islands, the mountains of Italy and the streets of Mexico.

Everywhere his journey has taken him, John has discovered a hunger among people to find a new way to live, with a yearning for freedom of expression. His belief that everyone has a book in them was born.

He is now a writing coach having worked with more than 200 authors from 40 different countries for the A Journey of Riches series http://ajourneyofriches.com/ and his publishing house, Motion Media International has published 20 non-fiction titles to date.

John also co-wrote and produced the movie documentary Adversity starring Jack Canfield, Rev. Micheal Bernard Beckwith, Dr. John Demartini and many more, coming soon in 2020. Moreover, you can bet there will be a best-selling book to follow!

Dr. Colleen Sabol-Olitsky

CHAPTER TWO

As a partner in a world-class dental office for 15 years, Dr. Colleen Olitsky has always had a passion for helping and serving others. A lover of exercise and self-care, Colleen has learned so much over the last decade about nutrition and how to achieve optimal health while aging gracefully.

These passions have ignited a fire in her to assist others in improving not only their physical health but also their financial health and mindset. Colleen believes that she has discovered the vehicle to achieve all of that and more.

Dr. Olitsky enjoys spending time at the beach, reading, traveling, and writing. She is the author of The Naked Tooth: What Cosmetic Dentists Don't Want You to Know.

She is married to her best friend, Dr. Jason Olitsky, and together, they reside in Ponte Vedra Beach, FL, with their children, Chase and Gabriella.

As a mother, healer, artist, yogi, ceremonialist and mentor, Nicole finds pure joy in empowering others along the path of self-realization.

Tracy Sotirakis

CHAPTER THREE

T racy Sotirakis, is an entrepreneur, makeup artist, hair stylist and educator. She is based out of Galveston, Texas. Tracy loves working her small business while also teaching others to be passionate about their careers and living their lives to the fullest.

When she takes time off, Tracy enjoys rollerskating, going to the beach, hiking, biking, and most of all, spending time with her loved ones.

Check out Tracy's website www.tracysmakeup.com or her Facebook www.facebook.com/tracy.sotirakis.

Jan De Smet

CHAPTER FOUR

B orn 15/7/1964
Koninklijk lyceum gent.
Koninklijk atheneum gent.
Social assistant stedelijk hoger instituut for sociale studies.
Criminology university gent.
Conscript Belgium army 85/86
Business career, owned about 50 different business from restaurants, construction companies, real estate, farming, fish farming, gyms, adult shops and other adult entertainment business's, etc…
Lived in France, USA , Russia, and South Africa.
Started "Work for a better world."
His children Myra & Arron were born in 1996 and 1998.
Migrated in 1999 to Australia.
Has been married three times.
Now lives on the Great Dividing Range, Northern NSW and Southern QLD.

Is focused on happiness and living self sufficiently in a small community.

Jan can be contacted via email :
devine.truth33@gmail.com

Susan Dampier

CHAPTER FIVE

Susan Dampier was born in New Jersey and spent much of her youth growing up in sunny Central Florida. A mom to six amazing children and three beautiful grandsons, she is a devoted mother and wife. Susan has always enjoyed mentoring and inspiring others. Still, it wasn't until she learned how to overcome the emotional addictions that she realized her full potential.

While working as a corporate professional, she discovered a network marketing company aligned with her beliefs and values and committed to developing the skills necessary to become a top professional in that industry. In 2018, she stepped away from a 22-year career in wealth management to pursue her passion for health and wellness and helping others on a full-time basis.

Later that year, she was honored to be recognized as the North American leader of her global wellness company and has built an organization of thousands. Susan and her husband Sean, reside in North Florida with their children

and enjoy spending time outdoors. Contact:
suz.dampier@gmail.com SusanDampier.com

Matt Bruce

CHAPTER SIX

Matthew Bruce is a former Australian soldier turned meditation teacher. With deployments to Afghanistan and with time spent with the special forces, he struggled to integrate back into society and suffered from PTSD for a number of years. Through a combination of holistic practises, he was able to rediscover his love for himself and others around him. He moved to Bali with his partner Ruth to take responsibility for his mental health and to heal his relationship with the outside world. Matthew's words are written from the heart and life experience, having only read a small number of books since high school. He has battled with poor written skills for most of his adult life, so his first book was quite the triumph and opportunity for growth. He combines several self-taught quantum visualizations and meditation techniques to help you upgrade your life and take back control of your inner and outer worlds. Matthew has tried a vast range of holistic healing practices to heal from PTSD. He shares his understanding and experience with freely available healing techniques and how they relate to Soldiers and first-line responders.

Matthew now teaches meditation and helps coach other soldiers and first-line responders. His intention is to help other victims of PTSD understand the steps they can take to improve themselves on the daily. Through implementing small changes and taking radical responsibility for our own state of mind, we can grow deeply and move through the trauma of the past. This will allow us to remove the anger we still hold on to and move forward with our lives. Once we understand how our minds are relating to the stress and stimulation of the outside world, we can use simple proven daily practices to create a truly limitless life.

Contact details:
Website: thrinvingwithptsd.com.au
Instagram: @thrivingwithptsd
Email: info@thrivingwithptsd.com.au
Phone number: 0406 700 050

Nicole Seeger

CHAPTER SEVEN

She awakened to the potency of the ancient healing arts after a near fatal riding accident at the age of 16. From there on Nicole started studying with many gifted intuitive healers, shamans and mentors of the Native American, Celtic and Zen Wisdom traditions.

Combining pragmatic modalities like psychotherapy and Trauma Release with different Eastern Healing Traditions and wisdom from a Yogic Path, helped her to leave behind a life shaped by over-achievement, a feeling of being underwhelmed, and burnout.

Following her passion has allowed Nicole to facilitate Personal Retreats,

One on One Healing Sessions, Women's Circles and Embodied Empowerment Trainings.

After leaving Canada in 2017 to travel the world and explore world schooling her kids, she now enjoys a laid-back lifestyle with her husband, two kids and dogs in Bali.

Being a true gypsy at heart Nicole loves exploring different cultures and countries while giving back to those in need.

nicole@nicoleseeger.com
+62 812-3829-2595
Instagram: instagram.com/soulfulnomadmomma

Carol Williams

CHAPTER EIGHT

C arol Williams is a professional relationship coach, family constellation facilitator, author, and creative storyteller dedicated to inspiring and empowering women to live up to their wildest and happiest dreams.

Born on the California coast in 1958 and moving to Amsterdam in 1982, she is a flip-flop wearing Dutch-ified California girl. She has two beautiful daughters and is happily married to her best friend, Ronald.

For more than 35 years, she has been a multi-passionate entrepreneur with an insatiable passion for personal development and helping others to reach their fullest potential. She continues to immerse herself in study with some of the greatest minds and inspirational teachers on the planet.

As owner and managing director of several businesses in the yoga, sport, health & wellness industry, Carol has mentored and coached thousands of women worldwide. She helped them navigate life's most challenging phases to make positive changes and feel more joy.

Her superpowers make people feel at home, humor, and the ability to always see the rainbow. She is honest, wears her heart on her sleeve, and will make you feel understood without judgment.

"By continuing to learn and grow, we improve our own lives and create a ripple effect in the world around us."

To book a free Clarity session go to
https://www.soul-essentials.nl
https://www.facebook.com/bysoulessentials
https://www.facebook.com/soulessentials1
https://www.instagram.com/bysoulessentials

Nicolas Perrin

CHAPTER NINE

Nicolas originally worked in the corporate world living the nine to five world and transitioned out ten years ago choosing to live a heart centred life. Moving from a survival mindset to a thriving one opened Nicolas up to embracing his gifts and living a courageous life of freedom.

Nicolas Perrin is a cosmic guide who supports difference makers to catalyze their most potent dormant gifts and live a life aligned to soul destiny. Nicolas supports his clients, who are gifted, to transcend the pain of playing small, confused about life's direction, and find it challenging to share their unique message with the world. His clients are supported through the creation of a magnetic vision & activating their divine soul blue print enabling them to make the highest difference in the world.

Nicolas believes in a holistic approach and shares about New Earth Paradigms, Intuition, meditation, energetic transmissions, somatic body transformation, soul driven leadership and a thriving mindset. He has been on his own inner awakened journey for 15 years and shares this gift with others too.

Nicolas has run over five hundred workshops, co-created with other facilitators and offered his work at conferences all over the world.

Over the last three years Nicolas has been living around the world visiting sacred sites and intentional communities. As a visionary, he is supporting to share alternative ways humanity can thrive in a win/win scenario with each other and the Earth.

Email: Nicolas@LionHeartCoaching.com.au
Website: www.LionHeartCoaching.com.au
Facebook: www.facebook.com/LionHeartcoaching
Instagram: LionHeartCoach

Jayma Lyn G. Day

CHAPTER TEN

Jayma Lyn isn't the usual entrepreneur. Her parents left the Philippines when she was nine, traveling to Portugal seeking new opportunities.

Looking back on her early years, Jayma Lyn saw that the worry and fears were the two forces that prevented her from achieving her own personal success. Conquering those self-defeating emotions brought Jayma Lyn a new perspective. As a result, she made it her mission to help others overcome worry and fear so they could achieve their dreams.

Her path was made explicit from her experience working with different embassies in the diplomatic community of Lisbon. For Jayma Lyn, taking that enormous business risk before she was 30 changed everything.

Jayma Lyn is a founder of A Diplomata (The Diplomat) restaurant. A Diplomata is finding new ways to meet consumer needs and bringing a faster cycle of innovation from the farm-to-catering and table dining experience. A Diplomata is creating new brands and products focused on unmet consumer needs. It's an international VIP dining experience for the diplomat, expatriate and gourmet foodie within the greater Lisbon area. VIP events live cooking workshops, Chef-crafted meals, and cooking kits made with locally sourced organic ingredients designed around dietary sensitivities. Guaranteed to make your taste buds travel, but the ingredients are local. Thought leader, she is also appointed Overseas Filipino Worker Family Club Portugal Chapter President, recently Filipino Food Ambassador in Portugal. For Jayma Lyn, taking that enormous business risk before she was 30 changed everything.

Jayma Lyn is a happy mother of two boys, wife, Chef, Founder.
facebook.com/mcsiemsen
Adiplomata.com

Peggy Liling Chen

CHAPTER ELEVEN

Peggy Liling Chen is a world traveller, a public speaker, Licensed Heal Your Life® Workshop Teacher, NLP Master Practitioner, life and business coach, and a writer. Through her promotion of the concept of Love Yourself, she has become a teacher and a role model for women who desire to create the life and career they deserve.

But before she started travelling around the world, she was from the family Chen, living in a rural area in Taiwan. Through the life lessons learned in the very traditional environment and the strong belief that men are more valuable than women, she was desperate for approval, which helped her gain more awareness of how to change her destiny and live in the life she deserved.

After having several successful careers in different fields – sales, marketing and training –, and practicing self-love and self-discovery with different gurus and teachers, Peggy decided her true calling was helping and empowering more women to believe that they have power within them to change their lives. She started her new business and created her new brand – So-Refreshing Coaching that it provides two main workshops of Heal Your Life® Workshop, coaching & NLP based Your Thoughts Have Power and Leadership Coaching & Training programmes.

Peggy's now living in Bali, the place she dreamed of living. She's running a project called "The Power of Women". She also has been creating a new online project – Learning for English Learning, which is aimed at helping and supporting non-English native speakers get along with their fears about learning and using English to create the life and career they dream of having. With an actionable methodology combined with the tools and techniques of Louise Hay's philosophies and the concept of Heal Your Life, as well as NLP, Peggy's mission is absolutely to support and inspire more people, especially women, to create and live the life they desire and deserve.

Peggy would be very appreciative and thrilled to have you stay in touch. Please get in touch with her via peggy.liling.c@gmail.com or Facebook: Peggy Liling Chen.

**"You gain strength, courage
and confidence by every experience
in which you really stop to
look fear in the face."**

~ Eleanor Roosevelt

Afterword

I hope you enjoyed the collection of heartfelt stories, wisdom and vulnerability shared. Storytelling is the oldest form of communication, and I hope you feel inspired to take a step toward living a fulfilling life. Feel free to contact any of the authors in this book, or the other books in this series.

The proceeds of this book will go to feeding many of the rural Balinese families that are struggling through the current pandemic.

Other books in the series are...

Returning to Love: A Journey of Riches, Book Twenty One
https://www.amazon.com/dp/B08C54M2RB

Develop Inner Strength : A Journey of Riches, Book Twenty
https://www.amazon.com/dp/1925919153

Building your Dreams : A Journey of Riches, Book Nineteen
https://www.amazon.com/dp/B081KZCN5R

Liberate your Struggles : A Journey of Riches, Book Eighteen
https://www.amazon.com/dp/1925919099

In Search of Happiness : A Journey of Riches, Book Seventeen
https://www.amazon.com/dp/B07R8HMP3K

Tapping into Courage : A Journey of Riches, Book Sixteen
https://www.amazon.com/dp/B07NDCY1KY

The Power Healing : A Journey of Riches, Book Fifteen
https://www.amazon.com/dp/B07LGRJQ2S

The Way of the Entrepreneur: A Journey Of Riches, Book Fourteen
https://www.amazon.com/dp/B07KNHYR8V

Discovering Love and Gratitude: A Journey Of Riches, Book Thirteen
https://www.amazon.com/dp/B07H23Q6D1

Transformational Change: A Journey Of Riches, Book Twelve
https://www.amazon.com/dp/B07FYHMQRS

Finding Inspiration: A Journey Of Riches, Book Eleven
https://www.amazon.com/dp/B07F1LS1ZW

Building your Life from Rock Bottom: A Journey Of Riches, Book Ten
https://www.amazon.com/dp/B07CZK155Z

Transformation Calling: A Journey Of Riches, Book Nine
https://www.amazon.com/dp/B07BWQY9FB

Letting Go and Embracing the New: A Journey Of Riches, Book Eight
https://www.amazon.com/dp/B079ZKT2C2

Making Empowering Choices: A Journey Of Riches,
Book Seven
https://www.amazon.com/Making-Empowering-Choices-
Journey-Riches-ebook/dp/B078JXMK5V

The Benefit of Challenge: A Journey Of Riches, Book Six
https://www.amazon.com/dp/B0778S2VBD

Personal Changes: A Journey Of Riches, Book Five
https://www.amazon.com/dp/B075WCQM4N

Dealing with Changes in Life: A Journey Of Riches, Book
Four
https://www.amazon.com/dp/B0716RDKK7

Making Changes: A Journey Of Riches, Book Three
https://www.amazon.com/dp/B01MYWNI5A

The Gift In Challenge: A Journey Of Riches, Book Two
https://www.amazon.com/dp/B01GBEML4G

From Darkness into the Light: A Journey Of Riches, Book
One
https://www.amazon.com/dp/B018QMPHJW

Thank you to all the authors that have shared aspects of their lives in the hope that it will inspire others to live a bigger version of themselves. I heard a great saying from Jim Rohan, "You can't complain and feel grateful at the same time." At any given moment, we have a choice to either feel like a victim of life, or be connected and grateful for it. I hope this book helps you to feel grateful, and go after your dreams. For more information about contributing to the series, visit http://ajourneyofriches.com/ . Furthermore if you enjoyed reading this book, we would appreciate your review on Amazon to help get our message out to more readers.

www.ingramcontent.com/pod-product-compliance
Lightning Source LLC
LaVergne TN
LVHW051501080426
835509LV00017B/1868